The Public World/Syntactically Impermanence

As: Nāgārjuna's "destruction of all philosophical views"—obviously this would include all modes of articulation, and any definitions or procedures of "discourse."

The Public World/
Syntactically Impermanence

LESLIE SCALAPINO

Wesleyan University Press

Published by University Press of New England :: Hanover and London

Wesleyan University Press
Published by University Press of New England, Hanover, NH 03755
© 1999 by Leslie Scalapino
All rights reserved
Printed in the United States of America   5 4 3 2 1
CIP data appear at the end of the book

The author wishes to thank Tom White for his helpful reading of this text in manuscript.

A version of "The Cannon" was published in the *American Poetry Review* (Spring, 1998). "Experience/'On' Sight" is Leslie Scalapino's part of an introduction to *SIGHT*, a collaboration by Lyn Hejinian and Leslie Scalapino, published by Edge Books. A version of "'Thinking Serially' in *For Love, Words*, and *Pieces*" was published in *Objects in the Terrifying Tense/Longing from Taking Place*, Leslie Scalapino (New York: Roof Books, 1993); and *Disembodied Poetics: Annals of the Jack Kerouac School*, edited by Anne Waldman and Andrew Schelling (Albuquerque: University of New Mexico Press, 1994). A version of "Footnoting" was published in *SHARK*. Passages from "The Radical Nature of Experience" on Philip Whalen appear in Leslie Scalapino's introduction to Philip Whalen's *Overtime: The Selected Poems*, edited by Michael Rothenberg (New York: Viking Penguin, 1999). A passage from "Silence and Sound/Text" appeared in *Boundary*.

A version of *The Weatherman Turns Himself In* was published by Zasterle Press, Canary Islands, Spain, 1995.

Passages from *As: All Occurrence in Structure, Unseen—(Deer Night)* were published in *Chain, Explosive Magazine, Boundary*, and *Fishdrum*.

:: *Contents*

Demonstration/Commentary

As: All Occurrence in Structure, Unseen

I could stay at home and I'd go out. There'd be a group of people in one setting or another who knew each other but gradually I began to feel withdrawn from them anyway.

It was easier to remember what had been said and I'd feel satisfied after going somewhere.

Other people seemed completely internal which I noticed when I'd observed a man for some time and saw that he'd say something about himself and I thought that he should be that entirely and that other people don't go into a sort of public world.

I wanted to be wholly transparent so that I would tell people details of my activities whether I was casual or angry.

::

I feel that the people I see are all right—in the sense of not getting very old—as I get out of the area where there are shops, a few houses.

I don't see them walk or move a great deal; and they wear good clothes or everyday clothes.

At the time a man doing construction work in the street comes in that slow delayed way; he is in a sort of public world, working for awhile. Then not working for periods of time possibly.

From *Considering how exaggerated music is*
Leslie Scalapino (North Point Press, 1982)

Demonstration/Commentary

:: *The Radical Nature of Experience*

Activity is the only community. The conservative gesture, always a constant (any ordering, institutional and societal) is to view both activity and time *per se* as a condition of tradition. As such, both time and activity are a "lost mass" at any time. "For just as modern man has been deprived of his biography, his experience has likewise been expropriated."[1]

My focus is on non-hierarchical structure in writing. For example, the implications of time as activity—the future being in the past and present, these times separate and going on simultaneously, equally active (in reference to Whalen's writing, and similar to Dōgen's conception of time and being)—suggest a non-hierarchical structure in which all times exist at once. And occur as activity without excluding each other. This is unrelated to social power (it can possibly transcend it) but is related to social intelligibility at some time. Social marginality is a state not producing necessarily, but related to, thought/form as discovery.

In Susan Howe's poetry, "vault line divergence" (dual marginality?) is tracking of observation itself as making a present-time.

Lyn Hejinian described to me her work in progress, *The Border Comedy*, as being instigated by the notion of a collaboration in which one sends one line to someone else and the other person adds to it; yet in *The Border Comedy* she writes one line, then allows time to pass and comes back to it. But she was having trouble making the line unfamiliar to herself. She couldn't get a line sufficiently unfamiliar, so began to work on all fifteen books of *The Border Comedy* (it is intended to be modeled on the fifteen books of Ovid's *Metamorphoses*) at the same time, perhaps only returning to one spot in the work a couple of weeks after it was written and only looking at a few lines on the computer at once (in order not to 're-member' the background). "In order to keep writing fresh the memory of it has to fade. Unfamiliar, it is 'of the moment.'"

In language horizontal and vertical time can occur at the same moment. Hejinian says that the unfamiliarity of the writing is a prompt; it prompts the future.

A lost mass (Paris gone)
Shine red in young swallow's mouth:

One of Philip Whalen's poems might be written over a period of several years in a notebook, then typed and chopped into separate lines, which, arranged on the floor, are comparisons of different moments or periods of time and his mind at those times. Thoughts would have similarities and differences in two times, say. "It is not collage," Whalen made the distinction speaking to me. Collage would be a completed woven or superimposed fabric (when read later); in his poems, the levels in the writing maintain their first imprint, the pattern of what the mind was doing at those different times. Is the distinction that a collage is more passive as a construction in the sense that the viewer sees it later, rather than active comparison on the part of the reader and writer in reading as real-time, an activity?

Whalen comments within *Scenes of Life at the Capital* that the process of copying from the manuscript to the typewriter suppresses the material: the copy is transmogrified throughout (with a sense of its original shape retained, its first imprint having been there); the physical original (written by hand in a notebook, before being translated into typeface) is also activity, it is physical imitation/which is fiction too. That is, it is fiction only; there's no original.

In Whalen's writing, comparable to Dōgen's articulation of being as time (the poetry not being a description of anything outside, but a demonstration of one's mind doing this—the syntax and structure duplicating the process that is the reader's own mind-phenomena), the nature of the present is only disjunctive; the times occurring separately are at the same time.

> Every place is the same
> Because I felt the same, remembering everything
> We boated for hours on the Lake of Constance . . .[2]

Remembering everything, all layers at the same time, writing *is* the mind's operations *per se and* imitation of it at the same time.

> Fits of psychic imperialism
>
> there's no point in returning until I find out
> why did I have to come all the way back here

endless belt of punchcards travels through the neighbor's loom
repetition of a pattern from a long time back

(p. 55)

Restatement adjusting perspective (also readjusting perception, which is pervasive, different from perspective) to an ordered sense is psychic imperialism; rather, Whalen is making overt imitation (in and) as being itself only the perspective's moment:

There is a wonderful kind of writing
Which is never written NOW
About this moment. It's always done later
And redone until it's perfect

(p. 60–61)

"I just want to wreck your mind." His moment redone is imitation rather than representation: he's imitating speaking to himself rather than the writing *dramatizing* conflicting postures (in the sense of posturing which is to portray his own psychology or conflicts). In other words, he makes constructions overt as voices simultaneously as their being the ego of the speaker. So it displaces it by occurring at the same time ("wrecks the mind").

Activity is everywhere not operated upon by only one. "No change of identity but a change of state" (p. 111). Activity is itself conditional.

That is, by placing passages of notation of events, seen to be similar and in the particular moment of text (construction of voices as shape/sound, their interrelation which is *that* moment—as being always outside the time when it occurred) there is a change in the shape and structure.

The poetry is ventriloquism that, by being sensitive scrutiny of himself, is actual conversation. The 'imprint' of someone only as their speaking has a shape that is the text.

Moment of change or connection is not coming from the individual (writer/reader) nor transformation from single crucial events, but is throughout the minute notations (isn't any of them *per se*, at any one time).

The writing as the crystal does not act upon or change anything:
. . . In order to make this day great
Yesterday must be altered

(p. 69)

Making "this day great" is at the same time illusion and observing the nature of subtle pervasive change that is not caused anywhere.

Being free of himself is tonal (he makes fun of himself, imitates himself). Speed and vision are manifestations of each other, an activity, being outside.

> Now currently appearing a persistent vision
> When it happens at the correct speed
> But if you get too close it is only
> Patterns of light
> Drop candy and try to follow it
> Creates new place and time.
>
> (p. 82)

Whalen cited *The Art of the Fugue* as an influence and described to me studying fugue structure, which is a pattern of major and minor melodies. The notebook method of composition of *Scenes of Life at the Capital* (capital cities of different times and locations are 'occurring' at the same time) is horizontal unfolding (procedure of the fugue) as note against note, and melodies moving over time as (if) 'history.'

In *The Kindness of Strangers*, excluding horizontal range, the horizontal is implied (it is excluded by at the same time being there implied, 'recalled'). Excluding this range by only 'choosing' the *non sequitur* (thought 'connection' omitted in close secession/succession) is disjunction in present time alone (that is, only the disjunction is there).

The implied 'comparison' (to shape/sound of horizontal fugue movement, as if 'history') is insisting on the process or act of that disjunction itself as *being* mind-phenomena.

Only the disjunction is there: occurring by the action (of the mind making leaps and remarks, and imitating its own sound and conversation, to itself or others); but there is the backlog at the same moment that is *range* itself. An implied vast space and terrain.

Whalen is saying we need not bear out the constructions that are in place. We are not 'caused' by 'history;' while it is being constructed.

Being "free from orders, notions, whims / Mine or other people's" is also to be free from one's own regime imposed even in 'procedure,' that of disjunction itself (or that he finds connection, makes a connection at all). One isn't remaining even in the moment of perspective as that 'disjunction' itself. The poem is one's always leaping out of one's mind, not being in the same moment of one's mind *there*.

"Olson told us that history was ended" (p. 120). The account of having been going to attempt to somersault, and the report that he had just somersaulted leaves nothing (no action). The writing 'records' actions, physical (mind actions, as if physical and mind were conflated as writing). To write as only disjunction is in order to "wreck" one's mind; a range having been excluded is entering the same time ("For Kai Snyder," p. 112).

Past, present, and future occurring at the same time (wreck one's mind) are the disjunction in which one cannot be in any instant.

Imitating the voice as melody in the fugue structure (not being in the same moment of one's mind) is history occurring as his own pattern ('found' by placing lines together) of past events, the writing repeating that pattern as connections, which are then new connections. The writer's 'own voices' are fictions of him and fictions of being voices, imitation only of conversation—which is what conversation is only. There's activity in that "All that I hear is me and silence."

> A lost mass (Paris gone)
> Shine red in young swallow's mouth
> (p. 136)

> STUDENT: "What keeps us from giving up everything?"
> TEACHER: "Fiction."
> (p. 135)

"Repetition of a pattern from a long time back," there is change throughout is history, so it's on nothing.

Writing the present moment, his activity right at that moment—'just what's happening' right now is a zero. People might get really bothered by his seemingly just writing about the activity in the minute, 'nothing.' It can't ever be a connection.

In *The Kindness of Strangers*, disjunction as timing, placing different times (dated poems and passages or lines of poems undated written at different times) against each other (melody against melody) so that the greater the distance the greater the disjunction/leap (or the opposite: the smaller the time distance, the greater the disjunction/leap. Leap is different from disjunction), then the disjunction or leap is not time?

Non sequitur as 'no relation' is used as differentiation; or similarity is used to be differentiation. Whalen is using *non sequitur* to be: not comparison but differentiation paired continually so as to occupy the same time, enter the same time. Contraries existing separately.

'Comparison' occurs by line as the nonstop weave/'history' in *Scenes of Life at the Capital*. In the dating of poems, with gaps of time, placed next to each other in *The Kindness of Strangers*, the writing is only the mind's process as if imitating the process, recording the 'inside' separate from the action in the world? "The act of remembering or the vibrations of the sutra / crash through the real world" (108): the 'act' and remembering—the two—*are* the action in the world, what it is only, and smash it by being in it; yet are in it, separate.

Vertical/horizontal: "All walking at some angle to this void reality / Immediate bright breath" (p. 108). The 'two' are together that are not two also:

> Morning zazen evening drunk
> Mosquito hawk legs thinner
> Than a leg between
> Legs thin as a
> Hairy laugh tail
>
> (108)

Compression of evening and morning in real-time only and being the same. "Cold penetrates the root of cold; heat penetrates the root of heat. Even if you try millions of times to avoid cold or heat, it is like trying to put a tail where your head is."[3]

The notebook method of *Scenes of Life at the Capital* (which is separate times compared to each other) allows all layers to occur at the same time in the text, while being read/acted in by the reader as real-time (representation) where it is not. It's only the way the mind works making fast disjunctions and connections; it is phenomena as being one's mind. 'Seeing' is not separate from being action and these are only the process of the text/one's mind phenomena. Writing is therefore an experiment of reality.

In *The Kindness of Strangers*, separate dated poems are placed next to each other out of sync chronologically: "Move without moving any THING."

Chronological sequence does not initiate (anywhere) in others.

The present only takes place 'now,' having no earlier occurrence, and is in the future which is not 'present.' 'Then' takes place 'now'; it was 'then' only when it occurred.

To explain eclipses and to predict them

large numbers are needed
most of all zero.

(p. 137)

So the "present intention" does not govern the future. "The crystal does / Nothing. Its shape and structure makes all / the difference."

A 'zero' (that excluding the horizontal range) is the disjunctive present, which is: 'then' is 'now,' the present is 'now,' and the future is the same 'now' (they occur at once, but not hindering each other, being entirely those times, separate from each other—in a 'present' as being disjunct).

As writing the 'present' is open or zero—a lost mass—as is an eclipse. One is not separate from activity anywhere. Or in it, either.

A minute move is there a *non sequitur per se.*

A 'random' (that is, detailed, minute) speck put beside (compared to?) some other 'random' (minute) speck—their interrelation occurring solely changes the entirety/interiority of 'historical' event (that which appears to be a crux and unified); the disjunction (in *non sequitur*) of the event occurs only as being that present-time.

The 'event' not existing at all and/as activity is throughout it. All times being brought together and separate simultaneously ('wreck the mind') is there being no 'history' *then.*

Comparing distinctions, which are the layers as states of mind in different times, as if these are the sound/shape that's the writing, is the 'interior' motion of 'experience.'

Susan Howe's "Otherworld light into fable/Best plays are secret plays":[4]

Second time somewhere—the second time is the present only
fictitious deeps
  Cries open to the words inside them
  Cries hurled through the woods—the moment of divergence is the physical page of the text.
  —their activity nowhere in it
  —*as* that being pervasive.
  in the otherday
  on wild thoughtpath—is throughout
  Moving the second moment, (of writing) into the place of the first moment, and occurring at the same time.—As the original moment

History does not exist; (my reading of her text "Articulation of Sound Forms in Time" is) Howe's writing is not a re-creation (the latter being 'drama') of people 'in history' but an occurrence solely in a present reader—that is itself the occurrence of disjunction.

Corruptible first figure—so that its second occurrence in/as present-time is itself only; is not transmuted.

The event (*Bright armies wolves warriors steers*) is not transmuted either, breaks bounds (is out of bounds) (p. 17)—*By* its being illusion—and is out of bounds by being marginal (real-time/historical) people who are 'unknown' or 'minor.'

Have lost the beaten track—being on the beaten track is one's illusion and losing it is. *Vault lines divergence*—the divergence occurs by the continuance of the illusion, the antecedent moment stretched and occurring 'only' in the present/as page of text merely, the written itself becomes the vault line and the divergence.

As their activity is nowhere in it—second figure can be somewhere, 'an' occurrence in time at all. That is, by history/event not existing at all, there can be occurrence at all.

The *Progress of self into illusion*/history as activity in the present only—because the real actions of the past no longer exist; *The figure of a far-off Wanderer* is illusion of self.

Whatever suffering existed then or now—is 'only' the present person in real-time; *Portents of lonely destructivism*

The line of writing as (their/any) one's physical death. As if the writing could be a spatial relation 'to' being.

The concentration is on *not* diverging from illusion—this is the physical/spatial relation that occurs as the text

The writing is also a false *Impulsion of a myth of beginning*, an element of *rigorous Americanism* as *Knowledge narrowly fixed Knowledge* (p. 12) by being antecedent to (any) action—it is nowhere—not existing in one—where one has no activity in the present.

Writing is the present creation of illusion in order to diverge from it in being a state of attention. Attention, the activity of reading or observing, is the only history and present moment—at all.

Best plays are secret plays (11)—because it is an action, at all (*Anarchy into named theory*) (p. 32)—this is in attention itself.

Her wild thoughtpath is there being a present at all—there's no life rather than activity there.

Frequently critics regard Howe's writing as salvaging 'lost' experiences in relation to tradition or history, rather than separating these (as actions) *from* history—rather than secret actions because they are not in history at all. Are also the actions that are 'of' that which is the poetry. Have no translation.

Howe's use of 'selection' (rather than initiation) as a writing process submerges the writer's activity of thought ostensibly in history itself, by being in prior texts by others outside one's/her own cognition as instrumental: "This is my historical consciousness. I have no choice in it. In my poetry, time and again, questions of assigning *the cause* of history dictate the sound of what is thought."[5]

Howe's introduction to her *Frame Structures: Early Poems 1974–1979*[6] places biographical accounts of people living before the author's life alongside memories of her childhood; that is, her life is 'unrelated' (can't be *observed* to be related) to theirs. Yet the framing of these accounts, and these being an introduction to the poems, structures a view of history as causality. Her framing there is 'opposite' from my reading of her lines from "Articulation of Sound Forms in Time." Her imposition of 'history' on her own life and poems is a traditionalist myth of beginning, a determinateness: "Innocency. A pure past that returns to itself unattackable in the framework. Restoration" (p. 26). A state that is "Innocency" suggests the poet's seeking stasis of a childhood reconfigured (as if a Golden Age). "Restoration" is that past state, which didn't exist and is desired.

Actions as Reading and Plays.

It occurs by simply giving up one's mind; yet one can't do that in order to write it. This contradiction is evoked also in reading and hearing it:
During performance of my poem/play, *The Weatherman Turns Himself In*, the audience sat in a darkened field of hanging black irises (flowers) with rapid action occurring outside this field in front of the viewers. The activity is going on in a medium where it cannot realistically occur. Rapid action is apparently being represented in a setting of a play that *cannot* be rapid action, as of action films; and the play's action is occurring solely via the language being stilled to be contemplative as the language's only activity.

For example, slab of yellow teeth man on motorcycle to slash woman hurrying with suitcase—occurs as 'speaking this action' at/in the exact time of it.

By the activity being separated from the language and going on at the same time, the action is not (only) what is heard and seen, and it only takes 'place' there.

Activity is the only community. At the same time the viewer is conscious of separation, one solely.

This passage from As: All Occurrence in Structure, Unseen—(Deer Night) (writing that is to be read and not enacted and is also the activity of a play) analyzes the structure of The Weatherman Turns Himself In:

There could be a circumstance in which the actions were continual and 'visible' by the people speaking of an action while doing it. People were describing an action as it was occurring and being seen: all being its occurrence. Being seen, seeing, and speaking are all actions that are equal and in time. A man said, "I found the action/the movements distracting—so that I couldn't listen—I just wanted to listen to the language." I want the viewer to exist, in this distraction. Not to listen as such. So as not to re-form the action of listening, itself. At all. That one could apprehend outside of formation only.

This same passage from As: All Occurrence in Structure, Unseen—(Deer Night) also analyzes structure in a prose work (of mine), Defoe, sections of which were performed as a play called The Present. In The Present, separate scenes occur at the same time in and at the sides of a small center space. The past action (which is the first part of the play; inconveniently difficult choreographed actions occur, such as a heroin dealer later flickering on a motorcycle being carried in a cocoon by starving boys on a desert) impinges into present commentary (second part of the play), the action recurring as a different present which is at the same time.

Thus both play (The Present) and prose work (Defoe) have sequences solely of written 'rendition' of physical action (in the play actions are 'said' as they are enacted) followed later by sequences of observation or discursive commentary (in the play this is in part two; these are spoken and also shown as handwritten phrases on slides): these are separate as if observing the physical actions, which are also past and present. The separated passages cause the 'obverse' (conceptualization or action) to collapse becoming one—always being separate. It is 'as if' we're seeing and reading mind structuring.

Writing not having any relation to event/being it—by being exactly its activity. It's the 'same thing' as life (syntactically)—it is life. It has to be or it's nothing.

"A child imitates in space certain motions and shapes derived from earlier incomprehensible relations conveyed by others. Motions are created beside (as if 'by') themselves, such as the motions of running." Actions are no more 'givens' that are known than are concepts. Thus, the text as imitation of physical movements/gestures (yet) *as language* is utterly separate from its conceptionalization. Both are empty in that the motions have no generalization (motions have no language, which is what they *are* there). For example, in *The Weatherman*: running is 'spoken' ("As from not being liked and so without there being anything runs") by The Other as she runs hurling a bar into the wheel spokes of cycles on which people attacking ride.

Conceptualization separate from action is observation of what? Occurrence does not bring these even with each other; so in occurrence (of either at the same time) they ('motions'—which *are* the occurrence—and 'conceptualization,' the occurrence) are utterly separate, are 'gone' there, and one realizes that.

Occurrence being separate from itself 'there,' "experience" is 'seen' from the viewpoint of its dissolution.

Giving up the outside as 'conversation' and at the same time giving up the interior 'conversation' occurs *in* the 'viewing' of performing (these becoming the same). 'Making' writing impermanent. Disjunct instant is neither conceptualization, nor "contemplation"/metaphysics, nor 'solely' action as in an action film (which is as if 'not' in life, the 'plot' of an action film being only segue of actions). Neither any thing *nor* its concept.

Agamben's notion of experience having been "expropriated," the individual supposedly no longer being able 'to have' experience ('they' say)—as one being separated from one's action and perception of it, or by their saying that this is so?—here ('viewing' text or viewing action as performance of it) the practice of separating occurrence as a form of attention—of there being no relation, of one to occurrence—is 'other than' alienation (renders "alienation" irrelevant, not what's occurring; rather, it is observation). Without being a message or polemics, this attention of itself as an activity is: 'watching the experience of one's mind at once as if 'with' one's physical actions—and watching as being itself action.' In other words, it reinstates "experience" as (separate from 'their' definition of one's, *or* one's own prior, experience) a different activity.

Notes

The Radical Nature of Experience was first given at a talk at the Assembling Alternatives conference at the University of New Hampshire, 1996.

1. Giorgio Agamben, *Infancy & History / Essays on the Destruction of Experience* (New York: Verso, 1993).

2. Philip Whalen, *Heavy Breathing* (Bolinas, Calif.: Four Seasons Foundation, 1980), 54. Hereafter cited in text by page number only.

3. Dōgen, *Moon in a Dewdrop, Writings of Zen Master Dōgen* (North Point, 1985), 108–109. Hereafter cited in text by page number only.

4. Susan Howe, *"Articulation of Sound Forms in Time," Singularities* (Middletown, Conn.: Wesleyan University Press, 1990). Hereafter cited in text by page number only.

5. *Postmodern American Poetry* (New York: Norton, 1994), 648.

6. Susan Howe, *Frame Structures, Early Poems 1974–1979* (New York: New Directions, 1996). Hereafter cited in text by page number only.

:: *The Cannon*

Political/Social Demonstration of the Time of Writing

The role of poetry in society is a secret doctrine—One is the visitor, yet the man reading first takes up most of the time. At a reception following the reading, a student engaging one, says, "It seems to me your work is like Gertrude Stein." The man, one's reading partner, immediately inserts himself and says, "Gertrude Stein. Certainly not! Gertrude Stein is the human mind—*she* [oneself] is merely human nature. [Reading of] someone dying of AIDS!" he scoffs. "*Her* writing is human nature, not the human mind," he instructs the student. At a reading with him a few days later, he insists that he will go first and "read for a very long time!"

Any interpretation or reference to this instance is merely experience/anecdotal, it is of human nature—therefore impermanent.

"As, one example, Godard's 'The immediate is chance. At the same time it is definitive. What I want is the definitive by chance.'"[1]

> the man's death—from
> being sick at a young age—as not a
> senseless point—not to—
> by desire—reach such a thing in
> that way[2]

This segment is from a long poem, *way*, in which each line and poem-segment is qualified (changed from within) by, and in, the entire structure of the extended writing. Yet the unplanned, forward structure is at once entirely changed by the minute, present-time unit. Real-time events 'recorded' (as only events as written, fragments that are sound patterns) were frequently so minute (with the exception of a friend dying of AIDS) that in passing, they could not be remembered later, had existence only as writing. Any event is qualified by the future even—in the writing itself.

One feels a sense of despair—trying to unravel a dichotomy that is despair. It's impossible to undo it because it is similar to the conventions that exist.

I have to unravel it as that is (one's) existing at all—interior instruction.
Yet someone else thinks that maintaining the dichotomy hierarchical is
existing—*for them.*

Seated in the audience, much of which is volatile—two men are to arise—
yet a destitute man is lying on the floor (he's come in because it's cold out-
side), he's stinking, only a few teeth, drunk raving, lying he has no arms
  drunk he can't hear their asking him to be quiet.

The armless is dragged raving from the room by a crowd of men and put
outside on the street. A young woman in the crowd comments that some
people, disturbed by this, are voicing "sentimentality."
    When one of the two men arises—an outsider, strong, frisky, who *has*
arms, also drunk, rises voluble and is dragged from the room and thrown
into the street—he returns with a huge lionish cat in his arms and says
"Look at this *big* cat" and is hurled through the door again—*One of
these men later says to oneself "And to think that you noticed this—there
at a time"* (one had written it in a segment—he hears it being read): *as if
one did not exist—as if only their existing occurred then.*
    He is no more responsible for that occurrence than oneself, although
he was regarded as 'in charge' of that context in which one was an out-
sider. *One as the outsider sees oneself as observing actively and at the
same time being inactive in the past event and the insider as active yet un-
observant there. The event itself occurs 'between' these.*
    *(My) intention—in poetry—is to get complete observing at the same
instant (space) as it being the action.*

There's no relation between events and events. Any. They are separate.
Events that occur—(regardless of their interpretation—). (But also that
they are at once *only* their interpretation and *only* their occurrence.)
    Radicals in the sixties and seventies used to speak at the same time
when authorities were speaking to change *what* the officials were saying.
    Outside(-events) is bounced to be occurrence. itself.

Paul Celan was described (I can't remember the source of this interpreta-
tion) as being essentially conflicted (just in written—or in spoken word

also?) in his own language, German being the language of the nation (his own) that had exterminated his people. (His written language was) articulation within the language that is seen to be oppression/to be separation from that which one loves.

The dichotomy is impermanence/separation; a distinction made, for example, by Bob Perelman, between writing based in the "experiential" (thus without authority or as the 'authority' of the bogus self only)—

and writing that is articulation of/and *as* social polemic (the writing of which is then regarded as not being "narrative"—the word "narrative" used as if that were anecdotal *per se*). Yet in the distinction there is an equivalence drawn between 'anecdotal' and formal innovation itself.

Two sentences from Bob Perelman's talk at the Assembling Alternatives conference at the University of New Hampshire: "This equation of social power, or say social intelligibility—the familiar—and poetic value challenges much of our poetics." "The equation is less clear in any positive sense, i.e., that social marginality produces good poetry."

The conception of a normative language as being dominant perspective (conception that there is such a dominant perspective; and that such is or should be determining) is hierarchical conception *per se*. I think that power is the poetic issue or narrative of this period. An aspect of the conflict broached in that narrative is: the continual transmogrification of gesture, making something into an intellectual concept that can't simply exist there, only the concept of the gesture respected.

In academic terminology, for example, there is now a category spoken of as "other," the assumption being that *we* are not that and therefore this area cannot be rendered, or even broached except from a distance. As if 'we' are of the world that articulates. The implication even is that if one is "other"—while a recipient of sympathy and elucidation, or lip-service—one being outside (as minorities, or lower class, at any rate experientially) has no repute or credibility, cannot speak. The assumption is that language be polemical or discursive exposition as it/one has no (or exposes there being no) intrinsic relation to the subject "other."

Yet that is one.

Distinction as 'doctrine' and 'experience' is the conventional social separation here; that is, it is the way our experience is culturally described. The other side of this coin (the camp of "emotion") bolsters the same view of reality but with an opposing allegiance: that is, the 'opposite' view (opposite from: ideology as basis) is that emotion/narrative/experience are aspects of "self" that, being viewed 'inherently,' appear not to be the same as (appear not to have any relation to) outside events. The personal, the confessional, is an "expression" of an inherent self as if that self were the *cause* (of events, of cognition), thus (in my view, and in that also of Perelman presumably) mistaking the nature of self in reality.

Yet either causal agent (self-scrutinizing 'conceptualization' or 'concept of personal self') are inaccurate as revelation of events—events' natures and relation to each other. "Stillness of that order, perhaps a node peculiar to the mind alone."[3] They are aspects of hierarchical categorization that merely duplicate that categorization.

Giving a reading from *As: All Occurrence in Structure, Unseen—(Deer Night)*, which is an intricate interweave, I included a passage, an overlay itself of seeing an impression (image) of blue dye on the surface of the eye only, dye that in fact in the circumstance is infused within the left side of the body of the person who thrashes being turned on a table.

A man speaking to me afterward referred only to the reference, in the writing, to the dye: *"that sounds like something that happened to you,"* *with the implication tonally as well as in mentioning only that point in the writing, it is thus inferior*
or that its happening explains the whole away.

it invalidates it by being experience

Bob Perelman argued (in his talk at the Assembling Alternatives symposium—attended by poets and professors from United Kingdom, United States, Canada, Australia, China, and elsewhere—at the University of New Hampshire, 1996) that contemporary poets working in 'experimentalist' modes have failed because their writing, by being its formal medium—(that is, cognition being changed by its articulation)—does not have "social power" (in that poetry does not communicate with large numbers of the public).

His argument and his own writing practice imply a writing based on the use of social stereotype as a polemical device—which thus eschews one's 'interior' thought/shape/motions articulated as motions/shape in syntax.

"Life opens into conceptless perspectives. Language surrounds chaos."[4]

In an exchange in the *Los Angeles Times* between John Ashbery and reviewer Alexander Theroux, Theroux declares:

I am unaware of shooting at any *bêtes noires* in my review of his [Ashbery's] books other than those [Pound, Stein, Olson, Zukofsky] who practice the crapulous and farcically self-defeating act of offering bad or half-made work under the guise of serious poetry to be pondered, when it remains in fact impossible to be understood. . . . Obscurantism is morally wrong precisely for the lie it tells in the pretense of coming forward with the truth it simultaneously—and always posturingly—refuses to divulge. . . . How can a poet of such byzantine contrivances miss my homely truth? Who should know better than he the moral and aesthetic bankruptcy of calling gibberish "poetry" or nonsense "modernist"? We have evidence he is able to write a simple line. What kind of modernist mind do we need to understand "Once I let a guy blow me . . ."

The notion of "communication," articulated as synonymous with power and as if a product with a normative format, is a slogan now at the same time that the schools and education are being contracted/denuded, to offer—to those who are not wealthy—curricula limited in informative, let alone exploratory, investigative content (such as history), that which is subject to conjecture.

Poetry in this time and nation is doing the work of philosophy—it is writing that is conjecture.

'Obscurantism' is related to the market notion of 'current history' (the effect—the 'social'—has already occurred supposedly) as cost-effective; the effect (of social power, or lack thereof) being assessed in present-time unrelated to the substance of occurrence.

Thought or apprehension—in this conception of utility—is not (to be) in relation to action which occurs (or as it occurs) outside.

All demonstrations (as writing or speaking) are sidetracked by being defined as a category. There's no answer to one as that would admit of something other into the conversation.

At a time when bookstores are closing, the market argument is that books are not needed because they won't sell. Barnes & Noble is receiving manuscripts from publishers to guide editors as to which manuscripts should be published based on projected sales. Big chains crush other bookstores, as well as publishing companies (Barnes & Noble's market advantages, and its selection against non-format books). "And the diluted formalism of the academy (the formal culture of the U.S.) is anemic & fraught with incompetence & unreality."[5]

The notion of defining 'the life' narrative as inferior is also defining what 'the life' *is*.

Defining is conceptualizing that separation of the public and 'interior' as power.

Writing may be discursive connections or stream-series of distillation of apprehension, the acknowledgment of its narrative being its scrutiny. The contemporary poetic-polemics association of "narrative" as being only convention—'experience' thus denigrated, not regarded as exploratory—in fact does not allow scrutiny of one's own polemic.

There is a conflation in leftist thought with conservative thought in devaluing writing/experience as demonstration/process (rather than doctrine-based). "Procedure" or formalism as modes of writing are embraced by both.

A characteristic of conservative thought is iteration of tradition for its own sake, valuable in that it *is* that. Social conditioning is transcended—there is no "other"—rather than perspective itself being seen being created. Without the conception of the social as phenomenological, actions that are rebellious in response to whatever conditions, are seen as 'personal' merely. Articulating outside's warp imitated as being one—is interpreted as one's being unable to comprehend, couldn't put things together.[6] A syntax that is this dismemberment will be incomprehensible in the framework of conservative thought (one characteristic of which: conception of the past as entity to be preserved as being the present). In terms of a conservative framework, 'dis-location' is seen as merely personal aberration or failure to comprehend the whole, rather than strategic and phenomenological.

Phenomenological 'dis-location' in writing is strategic and specific, detail arising from or noting social conditions or background; which conservative ideology regards as without transcendence, transient. Yet such transience is change as writing's subject (in avant garde or radical practices).

The view of aberration as failure is an exclusion that is an action, rendering what it defines as minor to the condition of nonexistent or irrelevant 'over-time.' (As if there were an 'objective' cultural basis that becomes or *is* 'history.')

Polemics was to be *demonstration* (*that was the intention*)—*yet now poetry is society's secret interior—thought's demonstration is scrutiny (there is no 'history,' because that is merely a description of an overview)—in that polemics-based writing merely imposes point of view and suppresses demonstration.*

Right-wing Republicans castigate labor on the radio by asking "how can 'our' society's labor compete while wearing combat boots?" That is, they should not have labor demands in order to compete in the world market.

One should dismantle protection of oneself in laboring *for* others in order to compete with outsiders—who can underbid one if employed *by* those others.

The attitude that the writing is invalidated by it being experience has its corollary—in the objection to there being in writing 'thought' which is at one in the same time as 'occurrence.' *Is* that occurrence.

This is what makes the present-time troubling, as Gertrude Stein said.

That 'one' is separate in occurrence (as if occurrence were collective) is particularly heinous to Americans.

Perelman (in that articulation of 'social power') is taking both of these positions (critique of and authority) at once, deftly enshrining authority—seemingly in the 'outside' as if *that* were causal. The illusion of 'occurrence' and that it is 'collective.'

'Social power' is the formation ('I') am trying to (*'must'*) dispel.

(The delineated cultural dichotomy itself 'makes' the reverberation in this last above sentence only 'extreme' defined as such [categorical terms such as "lyrical" "personal"—negatives from a radical perspective].

One can reverberate that ridicule itself [as echo of social] on oneself effectively *as* the writing-syntax—to 'bounce' it to be a separated *occurrence* also.

This can reveal something about 'one' in relation to social occurrence. And also the intention is to see what *occurrence is*.)

Polemical device as a writing process isn't to investigate shape and motion to find out what the event is—it is to instruct what one is to think about the event.

But the event (any) isn't even there (as that formation).

One/events can only exist outside of formation there.

People in this culture are ('described as' being) 'given' the view (as if view and description were an action, and as if it were causal) that they like that which is liked—if something appears *not liked* (by others) it can't have value. 'Separation' therefore is to be 'ridicule' itself.

As successful current poetic-critical 'theory'—a description of *itself* as 'radical' (left), which is at once sign and definition of status, is dependent on reproducing the conventional distinctions (as categories of thought).

The closing of bookstores and the utter commercialization of publishing and distribution indicate there will be few reading anywhere.

My sense is 'subjectivity'—rendered at all—is separation *per se* simply as observation of phenomena.

Poetically, this separation itself (delineated *as* writing, *as* its shape/syntax) is also a shadow (evocation) of that which is 'exterior,' the public.

Much of contemporary writing practice (of the 'experimentalist' mode) now is delineation (*in its syntax—i.e. it is gestural, an action*) of this separation of one. Writing now is being the 'interior' *and* the 'exterior.' To make these occur, *and* to see them 'real'-ly.

"We're not going to go on playing games, even if the rules are downright fascinating. We require a situation more like it really is—no rules at all. Only when we make them do it in our labs do crystals win our games. Do they then? I wonder."[7]

—*in one's conflict—in surveillance*—is at once interior and exterior. The 'directions' (as in a text of a play, in italics), which is the same as the rendering (as reading) of public context/scene, are the same as interior-speaking to oneself. *Writing to engage the interior of the writing itself, (which are then) as* exterior *events, for anything to occur—its motions change events.*

The discovery that poetry *has no relation to society*—I'd been struggling to maintain a relation. Yet writing's an interiorization (*not*/of that relation?). That is a separate action.

In a critical reading group where, in one meeting, writers were discussing dreams they had had, a man, having recounted (or read) his dream, whose connections and process were its activity said—*yet how could this (dream) be translated into a thought that was not personal, that was not the dream?* (to be made useful—in that it is not from oneself, not a mind action.)

Articulated only *as experience—an intense separation where there's no translation. If one speaks his language one can't be in friendship with him. Friendship having to do with extending across the social line or interior division where one has no power. Or it is that, one articulates a relation to him that is not related to power.*

My sense of relief that 'poetry has no relation to society'—is that one has despair in 'experiencing' that people have no connection to actions (outside, or their own)—even though these actions as if taking place 'secretly' change everything.

That 'poetry' (interior) 'has no relation' occurs as its being extended, as it is not determined actions by being 'those' (initiating in that space)—it has to be *continual* motions.

In a footnote to his book *The Marginalization of Poetry*, Perelman quotes a passage from my exchange with Ron Silliman, "What/Person: From an Exchange." In this complex exchange, (published in the *Poetics Journal*),[8] I was answering Silliman's position that women, gays, and minorities tend to write "conventional narrative" in that they have to "tell their stories," arising from their social conditions; whereas white heterosexual male writers (he says) are in a position to experiment formally.

The passage that Perelman quoted from my response to Silliman implies that I simply 'favor' "narrative" (whatever that is); that is, it reverses, erases the argument I was making by quoting a tiny passage out of context.

A person describing a creationist view that all minute events and phenomena are in God's eye or plan beforehand—so evolution *cannot* exist or occur—nothing is *occurring* first or apart from the plan—no actions are later events; astonished, I made the remark, "This is completely alien to poetry." Alien to observation, and also to action.

There is no cause or effect—the moment of occurrence doesn't exist either—in that the present moment is disjunction *per se* only (Nāgārjunian logic, which is early Zen, rendering modern physics?). All times (past, present, and future) are occurring at the same time separately *as that* disjunctive space or moment (rendition of Dōgen's and Einstein's sense of being as time). So occurrence is not hierarchically ordered. (These views of time and being are also [elsewhere] articulated as socially shared experiences.)

The language that is 'experimentally' based corresponds to people's *experience*; as the act of 'one's' experiencing; and (though not widely disseminated, thus not part of 'communal' experience) it is not an 'elite' language.

Doctrine doesn't reflect 'our'/their experience; is alien to it.

The contradictory, problematic factor is in divorcing 'experience' from 'non-referential' writing (originally with radical intention); a separation that sometimes simply stems from an attitude that 'experience' is lowly (that is, from snobbery and also regard for authority as opposed to demonstration).

One point I made to Silliman in the exchange was that the form of one's articulation may be a reconstituting of the general social narrative, may be a radical change in expression arising from one's *separation* from social convention.

Silliman's position was negating the factor of the individual's articulation as motions/shape in syntax *being* a radical change in thought.

In the early eighties, Silliman, in conversation and talks in San Francisco, urged poets to write syntax that was paragraphs without line breaks, paratactic, described as a communal, non-individualistic expression. The syntax has a recognizable sound pattern (which is what poetic syntaxes are, as from other periods, say languages called Beat or New York School). In the same spirit in that period, Bob Perelman stated, during a talk given by Michael Palmer on autobiography, that the erotic was not to enter into writing, the erotic was a form of ego to be stricken or omitted from writing. (At the time, this was related to a Marxist-based conception of writing that should be egoless: 'non-narrative' is *not* 'self-expression'—that's an action.)[9]

Roughly, paratactic syntax is juxtaposition to each other of 'unrelated,' which itself becomes a form of relation, statements or questions in one paragraph—a series of such leaps in continuing paragraphs or lines. A single statement is potentially examined or refuted by being in a series of such single 'unrelated' statements. This is a form of 'not holding onto a thought.' However, I think in order for the structure not to be deterministic, one would have to transgress the entirety—(as reader or writer) not be 'inside' the statements or questions having to respond to them. Either power or critique of it occurring as poetic syntax (of the time), 'one' must continually instigate—that is, one will write outside a 'given' syntax; not being defined by social articulation in any instant as syntactically.

There is no way in which women can apprehend conservative social articulation if they write uniform syntax (dictated by men) that excises the erotic.

One could not be separating the event—from/as thought (or apprehension).

Recently a man giving a (literary) talk showed slides of a 'pin-up girl'—interpreting the past to make the point that he thought she had a lot of "autonomy." The subject (pin-up girl[10]) has no writing 'as poetry'/*expression that's its writing*—and she's 'in' the past. *Granting those in the past, in their erotic being, "autonomy."*

Present as disjunct *per se* only—*that* space/time cannot be his narrative—or one's. *Event is between.* One has to modify one's tone if one is a woman to be heard as saying anything.

"To change without belief is anarchistic as instinct pricks from the Latin (stinguere), no law but that the absence of law is the resistance of love instinct with tact like the expression of this thought."[11]

Assessing relations of power between people—such as that say based in gender—merely becomes the articulating of those relations, as oneself having power. One would have to disrupt in writing one's own articulation of power at all.

A communal syntax being community could have occurred in an instant. When it occurs again, it isn't in the same syntax?

Format (when experiment becomes format) is not articulating occurrence (events/thought). It cannot, inherently. That is, those experimenting formally (as per Silliman's description) by accepting polemic directive are *per se* not practicing experiment—in that they are divorced from the live gesture?

The very nature of descriptive language is 'other' than the subject. What Giorgio Agamben identifies (locating it in infancy) as a silent pre-language state is going on at all times in one simultaneously 'alongside' one's language apprehension.[12]

("Experiment"—not as itself a brand of writing or as 'unfinished' 'attempts' rather than the 'finished product'—but as 'scientific experiment': to find out what something is, or to find out what's happening.)

In the view (such as in Anne Waldman's statements[13]) that (which is the real) poetry is "speech," there's a sense of "speech" (spoken is social, convention of 'conversation'?)—that is not "thought" [interior], is not 'felt spatially / such as correspondences in the limbs.' Tonal is considered thus as ranges of speaking voice or breath.

Yet poets have been writing other tones—that are in the written text only—tones not occurring as speaking. These are 'sounded' silently, spatially—a separation; between 'one' and 'social'? Or separation between 'one' and 'correspondences in the limbs'—and night. (As if a butterfly and the butterfly motion of a swimmer.)

We've mutated and become ventriloquists who speak 'inner' unspoken 'movements' and various types of speech at the same time.

I was interested in a syntax whose very mode of observation was to reveal its structure; that is, its subject and its mode are subjectivity being observation. Since it is itself subjective the viewpoint is 'without basis.' It removes its own basis, that of exterior authority, as a critique of itself.

As an example, sentences that are single, dual, or multiple clauses are only intonations, dislocating their 'interior' and 'exterior' subject—by one's 'interior' intonation and 'exterior' reference being the same (being a clause of the sentence, dissonant notes played at the same time) and as such also mutually exclusive, separately critiquing each other.

Statements of definition (that perceived as 'givens' 'in-coming' from the outside society, which 'determine' social reality) are apprehended as bogus. Because they are revealed as subjective, without basis. One is only constructing a reflection of these as one's reorientation of apprehension. The syntax itself reorients one's apprehension (by continual dis-location) and enables that which is exterior to be included in a process of its examination, necessarily self-examination.

My argument to Silliman was that no one can conceive within the 'given' language—and articulate reality, as that. It can't be 'there' because it *isn't* that.

This may or may not be a different concern from that of women and imported minorities working here as illegal indentured servants who are slaves, for example.

That is, individuals in writing or speaking may create a different syntax to articulate experience, as that is the only way experience occurs. Or they may describe their circumstances and contexts, as if from the outside, using normative language.

The dichotomy is in anyone as a function of the world? *Language as interior and entirely from the outside at once—which is a series, starting up throughout.*

"Holding to a course with the forbidden sublime, love of beauty originally obfuscates or sublimates to refine what is unclear to be scrambled later from its perception of perfection by that continuing. Which is to change the world. As it does which is why, nothing individually lost, there's a difference to be told."[14]

Notes

1. Clark Coolidge, quoted in *Postmodern American Poetry*, ed. Paul Hoover (New York: Norton, 1994), 652. My intention in taking all the written quotes from one source was to indicate the similarity of direction articulated by poets with widely varying aesthetics collected in one text. I was pointing to the existence of a commonality, which is 'public' even if not numbered in millions. However, Joan Retallack accurately pointed out to me that I didn't comment on the role in the canon of anthologizing: "A surface illusion of comprehensiveness gives these compendiums the power to conceptually blot out the possible presence of multitudes of other interesting writers and (in the case of the Hoover and Messerli anthologies) the small presses that publish them. I.e., they become a substitute (for teachers and writers) for going to the individual books of individual poets. That there are *many* anthologies of contemporary work coming out right now seems to me the only good sign. . . . Since the essay is entitled 'The Cannon' I immediately assumed you would be commenting on the way in which anthologies take over the reference market so to speak."

2. Leslie Scalapino, *way* (San Francisco: North Point Press, 1988), p. 105.

3. Clark Coolidge, in *Postmodern American Poetry*, p. 651.

4. Susan Howe, quoted in *Postmodern American Poetry*, p. 648.

5. Amiri Baraka, quoted in *Postmodern American Poetry*, p. 645.

6. "Everything is in the poems, but at the risk of sounding like the poor wealthy man's Allen Ginsberg I will write to you because I just heard that one of my fellow poets thinks that a poem of mine that can't be got at one reading is because I was confused too. Now, come on." Frank O'Hara, quoted in *Postmodern American Poetry*, p. 633.

7. John Cage, quoted in *Postmodern American Poetry*, p. 652.

8. Ron Silliman and Leslie Scalapino, "What / Person: From an Exchange," *Poetics Journal* 9 "The Person," pp. 51–68, ed. Lyn Hejinian and Barrett Watten, Berkeley, Calif., June 1991.

9. Bob Perelman doesn't remember making this remark and states he would not make such a comment as it is puritanical and offensive. It was not recorded

(the tape ended). His words were only *part* of an exchange in which a number of the men spoke, then agreed with his statement. No women spoke to this. He replied to this essay: "So I look at the picture of my literary position in your piece and see an inflexible anti-erotic commissar insisting that people write convention-ally." His point or remark to me here is well-taken: I do not mean to characterize his writing or thought in that manner, but rather to demonstrate occurrence in public expression of ideology.

10. Betty Page, referred to in a talk by Barrett Watten at the University of Maine.

11. Bernadette Mayer, quoted in *Postmodern American Poetry*, p. 659.

12. *Infancy & History / Essays on the Destruction of Experience*, Giorgio Agamben, Verso, 1993.

13. Talk given at Philip Whalen's Birthday Reading at the San Francisco Art Institute, October 20, 1996; and talk given at Allen Ginsberg's memorial in San Francisco.

14. Bernadette Mayer, quoted in *Postmodern American Poetry*, p. 659.

:: *Silence and Sound/Text*

Note on my work:

I would like to do a writing in which 'cultural' (that is, both outside one and interior) scrutiny can occur as being the process of the writer's thought and recognition coming up to the surface.

In *As: All Occurrence in Structure, Unseen—(Deer Night)*, I intended a double—that an outside culture as seen interiorly by one be brought to bear on one's own culture, that 'conceptualization' and 'experience' be at once apprehension and overt (as a play, yet read in silence) illusion.

This work was written during and after return from traveling in Bhutan and Thailand; it actually refers to many places, however. The word "their" sometimes refers to the people in the other culture, and more frequently to one's. I wanted to iterate the separation psychically (here), which would 'then' not be the cultural categorization, but the bounding out of 'one.' 'One' is maintained.

As if 'iterating' conflicts inside one and outside at once—it is motions' illusions.

'Their'/word has to jump into the bounds of 'their' location, as one-self; oneself interpreted as being or through their 'here' (one's own loca-tion)—one can be interiorly 'only' *other* than what one is.

The gesture itself and observing is recognized as illusion.

The attempt to articulate (this) itself is the separation:

"Notion that conceptualization and action are separate—one is not one

as bounding out of one—not as viewing *life* as inferior

to realign *their* narrative in the sense of the writing being that separa-tion—one is not one

as bounding out of one"

I wanted to use a particular tool: one, early, as a child, traveling having the sense of having no customs that are inherent—and reacting against one's own culture in its being obtuse force, and in its negating what is really there.

In that one is conflict only just as such—it is mirrored as one's interior.

It (one affected by conflict, and being that only—then) can't be articulated as that language—of the outside here.

Silence is that inarticulateness, a particular thing.

One is not articulating for others who have been silenced—or who are 'not heard' by 'history.'

Such a notion of history being reclaimed by expression is sentimentality —to be sympathizing with an other person in their past action, as if their being is passivity, erasure, or weakness. In a Hollywood movie about Burma, an American, witnessing the civil conflict, says that if what's happening there is not known and expressed in the West, "Then no one will know." *They* will know, their location, occurrence, and time having as much 'weight' as anywhere else.

Oneself is simply 'conflicts' or 'actions' as such. A surface. This is a relief because it can be changed.

(Not having been taught customs yet—early—traveling—these appear as only relative.) They have a spatial dimension.

The intention is that, because *As: All Occurrence in Structure, Unseen—(Deer Night)* is a play, yet the reader as one (isolated and enacted *by* it) reads the written words silently, the actions occur as if on its other side (as one sees the moon)—the actual exterior events, people on gorges streaming from overpopulated origins as immediate and past event, occur as a play's silent side only (occurring, enacted, by its being read).

Silence and sound both are as written text.

Yet this work could be enacted (by actors) to make an exterior of its own silent side. The events, as enacted, would have to be occurring at different times from when they were articulated (where they come up in the text)—a split—so that they would impinge on memory at the same time as their occurrence as contemplative *motions*.

The text being 'viewed' whether it is being read or enacted then.

The silent reading itself enacts social voices interiorly—as silent motions.

People are becoming unaccustomed to reading books. A man seeing a woman reading in public recently, came up and asked her, "What are you watching?"

The 'memory' in reading and exterior enactment (together) appears as if information, of events, though *viewers* will not have read it (but hearing the syntax gives them the shape of reading, the interior experience of reading), and appears to be one's own memory by being outside.—'Outside being free.'

Once, reading from this work at a poetry reading, some early 'memory' or reproduced event (stronger than "sensation" in that it had a sense of being complete) which I couldn't identify and holding me in it throughout, occurred side by side. The reproduced event or "memory," whatever it was, had not been represented, wasn't an event in *As: All Occurrence in Structure, Unseen.*

It was the folding (onto each other) of 'interior' motions (of different times), like being waved by a violent wave. It also gave me the impression of a lead into investigating what had been actually the grounds, the process as experiment, of this work. "Events" (always the "past") are a process. It's overt illusion of *outside's* relativity, changing a view of 'autobiography' to be vast 'interior' change in events.

As: All Occurrence in Structure, Unseen is political discourse by enacting the split between 'defining people's experience to them' (which is 'being defined from the outside') and 'experiencing as occurrence.'

It is a commentary on Shakespeare's *The Tempest* and *King Lear*, by being a total rewriting—that is, without using the plots, characters or language of Shakespeare. The writing is not a "lyrical" "meditation" on Caliban's colonized state. It is perspective that is rearrangement by itself (being perspective). Analysis takes 'the perceiver' into the most disturbing thing about the present (to paraphrase Stein)—as does being without analysis, being too close.

It's rearrangement of one's thought, by demonstrating its rearrangement. All the parts (and the entirety) of *The Public World/Syntactically Impermanence* constitute at once "critical analysis" and 'practice of demonstration of no-procedure.'[1]

The conceptions that are the writing are to be disbanded in it. Referring to my own writing and, separately, to hearing Mongolian Cyrillic: "Hearing the sounds, I couldn't be 'undoing' my culture by an (my) interior experiencing of theirs. Pronounced is in a different order from that written."[2]

There is no interior as 'them' or 'one.'

The writing being 'on' an early split in one's psyche is not 'about' one's psychology. It's a way of there being no difference between occurrence in the outside and as the inside. So that one is not separate from occurrence.

As: All Occurrence in Structure, Unseen is enactment of political discourse as it's being also a form of silence: people's expression that is not recognized or comprehensible as "discourse." It is expression that is excluded.

The refusal to be defined, by the action of out-racing 'one being defined'—and not 'being' that action either (of out-racing), though that's all that occurs—'to be' out racing (as a form of silence that 'isn't' 'inarticulateness'). Writing 'could be' leaping outside the 'round' of being interiorly/culturally defined (at all) (by oneself or outside)—yet language intrinsically can't do that?

Peter Hutton's Silent Films:

Sound effects aren't created by the viewer, no emotion is supplied (unless someone's doing that; in one showing of a Hutton film, a woman was sighing at the beauty, punctuating as if to supply a soundtrack, until someone in the darkness said to her from the row in front of her that the silence [as if a silhouette as a factor or occurrence itself—yet without being either a form of soundtrack by supplying a conception, or an absence] was not an omission, was deliberate so that one would not have background sound).

New York Portraits, Parts I, II, III:

The cuts (separating shots), the 'breaks' themselves require concentration on the part of the viewer, constituting an action of 'not seeing.'

Clouds and sky are given as much 'weight' as people—by the cuts between shots, and the delineation between objects being in darkness (different from the breaks).

People are viewed from above so that their actions, as their bodies also, are seen through as if at the center, a midsection from above.

Such as a man from above passed out on the sidewalk, wrapped by others who are seen through (the camera's view), the man administered to by them, and taken away in an ambulance.

Destitute people sleeping on the sidewalk or bench are motionless or a motion of a foot extended barely distinguishable, as viewing or silence, from dark ('night' or 'film,' the two at once).

Cars viewed from above occasionally wallow through a flooded street of illumined black water in night city, the same place (seen from above the flooded street) held for an indeterminant time.

A person in (plastic transparent bags?) wades through flooded street by building corner seen from above in day, separately by their self.

A crowd is gathered on the horizon as if a grainy-black sky a sun in it which is looking through them—with the Statue of Liberty on the other side past them—as a blimp slowly crosses the separation of the gray sky.

The silent dark as night or day where color is not relevant—and not separating them from horizon.

The blimp—in a different cut; that is, in another indeterminant shot and where the cuts between are as important as the held sight—slowly passes in the silence between the sides of 'thin' tall buildings.

People's language can't imitate what is seen/what they're seeing. There's no language (as if 'at all' or that interprets people 'there') viewing—or as what's seen.

So there's a total separation between anything seen and expression.

The viewer's activity of seeing is 'expression.'

There is a total separation between expression as 'seen' or 'seeing'—and the cuts, silent and contentless, without sight/site, yet requiring attentiveness.

There not being either sound or sight in the breaks/cuts, the activity of one's attention, in relation to just the *film*, is a terrain.

People seen being destitute, the limb of the person lying on the bench, is not 'expression.'

Really, seeing can't 'imitate' action. Or 'imitate' blackness terrain.

One's internal speaking there is not existing. Always sound/noise, by necessity, 'here' there is no language existing at all, either written or spoken. People are everywhere but are part of the existing calm endless terrain.

Notes

1. See "The Recovery of the Public World."
2. Leslie Scalapino, *R-hu*, manuscript.

:: *Footnoting*

A current genre—poetic discourse is itself 'poetry' ('theory' itself be-comes the mode that we regard as a new form of 'poetry,' whether or not it uses footnotes)—while having a radical potential, also proposes or is the opposite (similar to the Republican Gingrich packaging his conserva-tive views as "revolutionary"): a poet making reproductions (as theory) of other's radical gestures (making discourse that is radical cachet), claiming that that is the effect or gesture of their own writing as that 'the-ory' but without that gesture occurring. Without the gesture occurring *as the writing*.

Appropriation of ideas, even one's own—devoid of their gesture is the gutting of that. It is taken in some cases to *be* that gesture and celebrates itself being avant garde. So then the gesture can't exist? Because its ap-propriated form intrinsically is not what it is. It corrupts the gesture oc-curring by that being social success. In short, this proposes myriad ques-tions—when is 'the gesture' occurring?

So I am making a work in which 'both sides' exist, inseparable demon-stration and commentary—so that it may be examined.

In rewriting Shakespeare's *Tempest* without its plot or characters (the piece titled *As: All Occurrence in Structure, Unseen—[Deer Night]*), I 'imitate' or refer to an interior spatial configuration (irreconcilable oppo-sites existing as one/oneself at the same time—as 'one's' first encounter with the information of death).

Such a spatial configuration occurred at age fourteen returning from Asia and having to be reintegrated into American school life which had also the interior 'trace' over it of sense of the extreme suffering of people inescapably, causing one to 'flip out.'

The events that in the present triggered the writing of *Deer Night* were traveling to Thailand and Bhutan (in Bhutan, standing on a ledge on a cliff watching for four hours monks perform the Bardo dance, which is 'on' one's negotiation of entry into and emergence through death; at the moment of the whirling figure of Death entering, Westerners ran sticking their cameras in the faces of the bystanders/audience who'd entered the dance bowing to pray, the Westerners refusing to withdraw at the request of the Bhutanese police; at this, shocked waves from the small children who were standing on my feet to look down as if flying out on the cliff ledge). Returning to the United States, an immediate interior imitation of the same spatial configuration (as when a kid) briefly recurred by, as it happened, people in a social event describing split between intellect and emotion (in that case validating intellect), convention to which I'd responded earlier as a kid—which by that split being conceptualized as if by 'society' made existence outside it impossible (felt as untenable, as suffering). Yet there was no existence within it.

It was not integration (of emotion and intellect, or integration into society) that was needed, but rather iteration of configurations that are then there, single—to be existing outside 'society.'

Description that re-integrates this conflict into conventional categories of "psychological," "personal," or "metaphysical" only 'drives' the conflict into further iteration—so to be accurate it can only exist as its conflict (since that would be being outside one). By our cultural standard it will then constantly be redefined to be "oneself."

The placing of a point of observation not only on (or from) oneself, but on an earlier self no longer existing, by our cultural categories (and, differently, in Nāgārjuna's view also[1]) renders that point groundless. It's memory of spatial movement. This is the only recovery of the public world.

In a collaboration, dance with text, one person moves silently (gestures that do not illustrate what is being said); while another reads a text and walks at the same time as reading (the act of reading is not an illustration of the text's substance but itself a movement) in relation to the 'unknown' physical movements of the other. The one making sound (a form of music for the other's dance), walking goes through the process of reading, rather than speaking after memorizing which would be 'dramatization' or performance. (This is a description of a collaboration between dancer June Watanabe and myself, using part of my text, *New Time*.) It is 'about' time in that a new time occurs outside as being the present moment 'then,' which is separate from either the text or the interaction between the people (and separate from the interaction between one's reading and one's present mind) but arising 'between' these.

As written text (of *New Time*): the text is phrases separated by dashes which simultaneously relate and dis-connect (also, the phrases are simultaneously unrelated). The phrases are 'as' (the motion of?—by being separated, 'other than') 'being in the place of'—freezing-red-sky-dusk-that-is-dawn. There is no relation 'outside.' At all.

Dawn is at the same time as dusk 'as' present time. Syntax 'there' (of the text) is relational as if a 'time' of (*because* 'other than'—as it does not reflect) (is occurrence of) muscular physical motion (such as people hurling their frames on a wall, or one cognizing iris blossom in the air). It is a 'time' not as speech or sound *per se*—but as the reader's experience of simultaneous relating and dis-connection only. There is 'to be' no basis.

The gesture of *Deer Night* is: As one—first encounter with the information that death is inescapable—leading to 'flipping out' to be disruption *per se*, which therefore cannot form a conclusion either.

This is 'completely' illusionistic (the self, whether reader/viewer or writer, being the act of observation—being alongside itself); the iteration of the event of fear as separation from action, as *being* that action, is itself the illusion and the indicator of illusion. The notion being, this would not allow any procedures[2] or repetition.

It's the harrowing of one's own mind—to be others—as if throwing it up as a shadow of one's physical husk, and that in the same place where the moon is actually.

In (*Deer Night*) rewriting *King Lear* at the same time (as *The Tempest*, that being 'on' the omission of others, not having been 'allowed' their 'self'—such as Caliban, who is not-related [which is an action] in the rewrite to the Ibex)—the information is that Lear "hath ever but slenderly known himself" demonstrated by Cordelia telling him the truth, oneself telling oneself the truth.

Loving chameleons, where one has been deluded (relation to power), *is* actually love, (by being) in the process of its nonexistence.

Conservatives aren't being accurate. (That's a *definition* of conservatives.) 'Thinking' would be (if it were occurring) trying to see what is there, what's happening. Rather than trying to enshrine by description.

The mind does not simply imitate (one's own experiences, or language patterns one has read)—there is the moment of impermanence—that (when it) is something else. It has not occurred before. This is the exciting moment. One has forgotten what has occurred.

To produce this impermanence by iterating dissimilarities until they become something else—is the opposite movement of (converse of) obsession or imitation.

Notes

1. See discussion of Nāgārjuna's views which are intended "to do away with all philosophical views" in "Recovery of the Public World"; and C. W. Huntington, Jr., with Geshé Namgyal Wangchen, *The Emptiness of Emptiness: An Introduction to Early Indian Mādhyamika* (Honolulu: University of Hawai'i Press, 1989).

2. Wouldn't allow this approach in the sense of designating a procedure, which is therefore fixed.

:: *thin-space*

(*Zither* has a prose and poem beginning; and ends with poems that are without narrative or reference to that earlier narrative. The prose narrative is, in its splices of characters in actions, like a comic strip; the boa dove is one character—she's being harassed by brownshirts, as are all the citizens; the Mayfly, another character, is a minion of the brownshirts. There is a girl with beautiful arched eyebrows who frees a horse that is being beaten by a crowd by riding the horse out of the crowd.)

Last night I was having a conversation with a poet on the phone in which she said, words to the effect, 'children think in such-and-such way (conception that their development is the same)—they do not think that things aren't making sense; whatever does not "fit into" sense to them they discard as irrelevant.'

Children were in disruption. We are those. They saw it was disruption, which is what? Studies of the brain suggest that we make visual, physical sites in the brain of new phenomena we encounter (whether or not we understand it?); they are locations. Children do not discard new locations, they see them again later?

The chronology and space of *Zither* is a prior site/sight—we don't know about thought. We don't know how we think—not being an entity—or what development is.

So there is apparently not a relation—or it is unknown what the relation *is*—between the prose that is the beginning section and the end section that is poems. The split between them is a thought, occurring 'by' that split. The 'early' is acted upon; 'early' occurs throughout.

Zither has to do with the relation between past events (or present events) and thought; this is a reverse of order in both time and structure: in other words, there is no relation (?) between the two based on cause and effect (which is 'description')—in that 'outside' events are not within one's control *or* apprehension, because an occurrence is infinite (events being warped fictionalized are not, *and are*, 'subject' to thought). In the same time.

I'm putting them in the same time.

The utter freedom that's *one's* meeting/'to'/being in the event—prior—and after—at once, where there's no difference—is *his* early walking.

Before early walking—is early walking—to (too).

In the writing—the relation of a spatial middle ground that's the same as a vast exterior space-terrain is demonstration itself.

What difference does it make how children perceive? We have to think now to anticipate earlier child—'to make' no relation to them. Or one, to have no relation to one.

I don't mean memory, rather thought as both a past and present action. Past in that events may be forgotten, but continuing (or having a relation as impermanent). Cause and effect is 'our' conventional conception of thought, and is our *process* of thought (we do these conventions of thought in order to think—not that thought doesn't have a physiological basis, but we don't know this basis and it also changes, so isn't a determination).

Also, description or 'commentary' does not change the (text's) later motion (of the poems in the end section); interpretation (either early or in present-time) does not override their present motion.

So I'm making outside events 'subject' as an action to one's thoughts, any, (by putting them in the same time) and as such setting them loose, stacked space, 'outside' and 'interior' at once, a(ny) change in spatial conceptual shape. The shape is thought/relation to/'historical' occurrence.

Trying to see how thought occurs.

Changing the past events by thought acting on them, not simply it having a new relation to them.

The prose is top-heavy.

One emerges into the forest on one's one-wheel bike meeting for the first time others—who are (by their description) like oneself.

Also the split between the two is 'early influence'; in this case my sense of early influence of 'Asia' on difference between here and one. Here being U.S. culture. While taking into account that at every point one sees in terms of and as interpretations (philosophy one learned and accepted),

the writing doesn't have a philosophical basis except that of 'experiment'
per se—'on itself' as *being* the relation to the outside. One's apprehension
is being prevented from 'representing' the outside—by emerging into the
forest floating on the one-wheel bike—and couldn't possibly be doing so
(or be it).

    thin-space in which one isn't apprehension in 'that' either.

his
planks as dawn [heart's valve — rungs] — goes on
        opened so people's leaving camps
at night
people's tendons being hacked in many — in
        along —
in planks [his — dawn] leaps one him their — to side

        night
        base — there is no base

        ————————

        breaks past rungs while in their middle —
dawn's
        his — people's — fleeing camps — one's
bursting — 'in' it — separate — is — on his

        his quiet's
[[his] 'heart's' — valve] burst 'on' — a — dawn time — one's

:: Experience/'On' Sight

Sight is a collaboration between Lyn Hejinian and Leslie Scalapino. After its completion both separately wrote descriptions of their process. The following is from Scalapino.

From: Sight:

The head of the pink tulip, bunches of them fully open are blind—and aren't born; are eyeless and not born, or are born and are in fields where one cow is blowing
     It moves in the field whether it's disturbing them; they're not born and are existing anyway, it moves in them
     They have this peaceful but wild existence—where everything's disturbed in it, but not by them
     if the cow's behind it doesn't suffer and is observant, the tulips not being born (bourne) and being pink rushes

     The Red Sea not to see filled with the violent pink rushes sustains the cow to have it wade, to have it walk."

We agreed that the form of our collaboration was to be in doubles, pairs (such as two sentences, two lines or paragraphs, or series of these, and so on); and that the subject, being sight, should involve things actually seen. Multiple pairs and crossing the borders of these occur: which are friendship/thought/sight itself/events . . .

     Crossing 'across' observation, 'argument' which is mode of extension—we tend to stay on our own 'sides' in regard to the 'subject' 'experience.' We attempt to draw each other across the sides of our 'argument' or boundary, a form of pairs, and of friendship also. We sign our segments (the above being one of mine), which are sometimes like letters as specifically referring to occasion and to writing. 'Critical discourse,' as they say, in which the poetry is interchangeable as the thought in it. Sometimes, seeing in real events we had to turn seeing up to an extreme in order to see it, as if dreaming, being suppressed, were bursting out as luminous seeing in the waking state. Pairs of sights, become that by being placed beside each other; my dreaming speaking to you (a pairing of you), I put in as part of the collaboration.

Friendship would have to be not just 'being liked.' That one has to be likable, accommodating. One would have to 'like' also—that is, like the other—and I think only *by* being oneself. Not accommodating. My need for argument in it is that you tend to view reality as wholesome; when I'm suffering you tend to alleviate to bring suffering into the currency of the 'social,' the realm that is convivial—whereas I'm saying it's (also) apprehension itself when it's occurring.

The accumulation of pairings as 'extreme' sights occurs to the extent of being as if the writing's faculty, rather than being imaginative images.

I dreamt while we were collaborating that I spat in a donkey's eye (in the future, but already known) and rushed up (before this) to tell you that all of life was void, which I knew in the dream you would want to hear. Because I was indicating that to spit in the donkey's eye (not to have to be accommodating) was the gesture, being done; that gesture also being the act of friendship and apprehension.

So, anyway—I tend to say that experience is scrutiny; that it is 'travel' in the sense of dislocation of one's own perspective (that is, not to have a perspective). You say to me then: "travel is sentimental." In other words, I'm deluding myself that I could ever not have a perspective. It is my 'doctrine' only. (You're right. I agree, it was not scrutiny enough.) When I 'discuss' "compassion," you check me. That such (in that form at least) is egotism or a 'lyrical illusion,' probably.

Then, on my part, I thought recently you described (at the university) your writing in terms of ideas—that it is "comparing cultures"—which will be accepted as description of the writing (its importance) but which are not the gesture that occurs *as* the writing (the mind coming up with whatever it is at that moment only). (Acknowledgment that it is perspective only.) Because you know the professors will tend not to like the 'idea' of the mind and only its action at a moment, because they don't trust that. It isn't 'any thing.' 'Writing separate from and being then people's activity' is one of the subjects of *Sight*.

As doubles or pairings: the description as what people will like is not the way the thing (the event or writing) *is*.

The writing that's occurring at any point is the entire body of writing. Of others, as well. So the writing of a time is everyone.

A 'time' is the work being written at the time by everyone. It is not the hierarchy of what people regard.[1] In that accumulation transforms.

I want friendship that's real, because it occurs only. (This was Lear's mistake—or maybe it was Cordelia's—?—they seem to be part of the same person. I was rewriting *King Lear* in a recent work of mine, called *As: All Occurrence in Structure, Unseen—(Deer Night)*, which I was doing alongside *Sight*. I was also writing *The Front Matter, Dead Souls*. Passages of mine originating in *Sight* got into *The Front Matter* as being alongside it. In the latter, I was working on visual extremity as the writing literally as if a faculty, rather than visual being imagination.)

In such an approach—(if there's a division between description and text—you're pointing away from there being a text, from reading) you're not comparing cultures because you're indicating in a sense 'the real' is 'the social,' what is liked—else it is lyrical illusion.

Yet, to be "comparing cultures"—cannot occur from a standpoint that is an insulated one in which reality is described as (one's) halcyon/ "normal" (by such description regarded as objective in regard to culture and thought, as what is seen to be "intellectual" *per se*). Comparing cultures cannot occur as that, reality or cultures not being subject to 'halcyon'/'normal.' Apprehension as comparison isn't there then, because it's generalized. Were it there, that would be dis-locating. It (apprehension/conflict—the same?) isn't there. The point is not that one is suffering because of being dislocated—but that the thought *is* the action.

So you're (one's) 'being removed from experience' as that *being* (if that's one's) definition of objectivity or apprehension itself—whereas apprehension only *exists* as experience?

Note

1. Say, the anthologizing process is to leave out the time everyone is in—that is what the anthologizing process *is*.

:: *'Thinking Serially' in* For Love, Words *and* Pieces

The social conditions in which the courtly love poem arose were such that relations between people are convention. If one is looking at relations between people in their writing, that is convention—as the writing's form.

Creeley uses the form as inherent conflict by its being (only) present time.

His particular circumstance or place (in the poem, as notation of place), the factor of being in it, does not allow convention. One's only existence is in conflict *per se*. The being of 'one' is conflict. He sees the real as only the present.

Poems in *For Love* use the convention of Elizabethan love poem or quality of medieval courtly love tradition, written as Creeley's present time: as that is what is actually occurring (in the conception of marriage; or the courtly conception of the idealized love, which is outside of marriage)—the two continually separate. *For Love* is a serial work because it is inherently conflict that starts again and again: it has the quality of being precisely that which is its form; so the 'theme' of the poems is its form.

> Moving in the mind's
> patterns, recognized
> because there is where
> they happen.[1]

Creeley's 'two' who are separate are sometimes the lover and his lady, or two ladies, one in the lover's mind and one in reality; or the lover himself who is double split internally as being both the lady and himself.

> I know two women
> and the one
> is tangible substance,
> flesh and bone.

> The other in my mind
>   occurs.
> She keeps her strict
>   proportion there.
> (CP, "The Wife," p. 252)

Delineation of the conflict is the form of the poem.

> In the dream
> I see
> two faces turned,
>
> one of which
> I assume mine, one
> of which I assume
>
> . . . .
>
> If all women are
> mothers, what
> are men
>
> standing
> in dreams, mine
> or theirs,
>
> empty of
> all but themselves.
> They are so
>
> lonely, unknown
> there, I run
> for whatever
>
> is not
> them, turning
> into that consequence
>
> makes me
> my mother hating
> myself.
> (CP, "The Dream," p. 298)

The only description is the weight of the measure itself, the tracking that is the poem. The poem is serial because it is its measure. The poems are a series because they are separate and continuous. There may be a reversal of what's actually being said, the form of experience:

> I will never get there.
> Oh Lady, remember me
> who in Your service grows older
> not wiser, no more than before.
>
> How can I die alone.
> Where will I be then who am now alone,
> what groans so pathetically
> in this room where I am alone?
> (CP, "The Doors," p. 201)

Position in ordering (from the reader's perspective, or writer's, of the serial collection) is arbitrary; perspective is no ordering. "Position is where you / put it, where it is" (CP, "Window," p. 284). That's why he would die alone: the shapes that one creates do not mimic reality, but appear with reality, are part of it. One can't be united with one. (I'm reading *For Love*, *Words*, and *Pieces* as chronological collection, not considering these as separate 'books.')

If perspective is no ordering, the chronologically ordered *Collected* is a range and configuration of potential, infinite actions which are on the edge-of-seeing their actual occurring (by *being* chronological). The shape and movement of the real past event—which was as that time's present—is activated in configurations continuously.

The senses recreate the particular place which is then closure of that place (CP, "Variations," p. 288). The individual component of the series is not description ("I do not feel / what it was I was feeling"); and therefore the 'place' does not exist once it is over and the writing must begin again. The courtly love poem is a recurring address to the unobtainable; serial thinking is what Creeley's poem is beginning in *For Love*. It's articulated as the 'two' that are separate and a series: "in its feeling, / two things, / one and one" (CP, "Song," p. 319). (I'm considering the numbers 'two.' A series of numbers, moving the center off 'two,' occurs in *Pieces*.)

The terms that courtly love convention posits are that one's being is possible only within those courtly terms: in impossible union. For Creeley, one can never equal one. Being absolutely in the present and absolutely separate from it at the same time:

THE WINDOW

There will be no simple
way to avoid what
confronts me. Again and

again I know it, but
take heart, hopefully,
in the world unavoidably
present. Here, I think,
is a day, not a
but the. My hands are

shaking, there is
an insistent tremble
from the night's
drinking. But what
was I after, you
were surely open to me.
Out the far window
there was such intensity

of yellow light. But love,
love I so wanted I
got, didn't I, and then
fell senseless, with relief.
                    (CP, p. 336)

The mystery of that being (it being that form) is union.

The union isn't the love.

It's a space or 'inner' configuration that's unknown and to which the love is articulated.

Creeley's writing in these works is in continual conflict between an overriding conception, and the process that is being within the series and not seeing what's ahead: "is an event only / for the observer? / No one / there" (CP, p. 379). Creeley, in *Pieces*, is moving around in what he characterizes as an American quality of event or mind: having no overriding conception, continually resisting such, which itself creates it.

Americans have a funny way—
somebody wrote a poem about it—
of "doing nothing"—What else
should, can, they do?

                    *

What
by being not
is—is not
by being.   (CP, p. 406)

That hole ("When holes taste good / we'll put them in our bread") is merely a component of that place (of or in the series). The theme of hole or circle, sometimes delineating seeing only within the mind's own forms repetitively, or an emptiness (*not* repetitive) that is joy (*Words*: CP, "The Circle," p. 343; CP, "The Hole," p. 344; CP, "Joy," p. 350) is only the particular articulation of those spaces there (in the series) as the number zero.

The fixed place or the place that is recreated by the senses and thus closed, is the point of being separated from the present. It is where: *They* were imagination, and the *world* also; the rules known prior to be wrong—then the mind followed and I also as it was true. Phenomena has to be ahead of mind. It is the 'ground of people,' the place or relation between people as the form of the writing, the converse of definition *by* place (as in "The Puritan Ethos" [CP, p. 414], the geographical mind space that displaces the "other space" that is "several/dimensional locus").

The "several dimensioned locus" is the serial work that is really all over, multiple. It occurs in the ground that has been excluded by the conception of 'higher authority'/Puritan ethos (our *actual* social construction), for which work, the visible result and activity, *not* the relationship between people, exists. These 'relations' as such (that is, if they are occurring) aren't hierarchical, except when *interpreted*, which is through convention of that hierarchy. So they don't exist except outside it.

If erotic love is knowledge to be traced occurrence isn't ever seen.

As in the courtly love tradition of relation to the unobtainable, the dual consciousness of the 'Puritan heritage' is to be transcended. The autobiography, the 'life,' in this society is to be obliterated. The 'confessional self' of writing is a format, so it obliterates the 'real.' Creeley is obliterating literary 'confessional self' by the 'life' being.

In the poem "The Windows," 'reaching' (or being in) love is being in *the* day, the unavoidable single present world. If "They"/American/or Puritan ethos are imagination and the *world* also, they are constituting a geographical mind space that excludes the possibility of that relation with people (that of being in the unavoidable single present *world*).

The Americans' funny way of "doing nothing" is such being in the single present world. The "several dimensioned locus" of the serial writing is not planned or composed, which is ordered in advance. The components/individual poems of the 'series' (the three works read as chronological collection) are delineation of that mind space of that particular poem as it occurs.[2] In-so-far as a poem delineates the conflict of 'convention'/of 'love,' for example, the poem is literally the presentation of the "mind's

patterns"—rather than a hierarchical imposition on that mind space sub-
stituting social convention as the point of view (CP, "The Dream," p.
298). Poems in *For Love* and *Words* using courtly love conventions/as re-
flection of American/or Puritan ethos space, as serial thinking are "doing
nothing" in the sense of being in the single present world only where that
very *convention*/of love is not taking place. "By being not / is." (Serial
thinking, "doing nothing"—not anything 'only'—is the present time.)
Americans doing nothing is the converse of their own living in conven-
tion—these 'two' occurring as 'at the same time' (place, placed as time).

The mind's patterns contain convention (habit) and repeat it but do
not remain in it in the serial writing, though it is a race to continually
move off of the dead center that is its formation:

> Quicker
> than that, can't
> get off "the
> dead center of"
>
> myself. He/I
> were walking. Then
> the place is/was
> not ever enough.
> (CP, "A Sight," p. 340)

The mind space that is 'created' that is the form of these poems is the ge-
ographical space of that love; where one is most oneself, and thus alone
in the heretical sense/of our Puritan ethos.

It is actually where relationship between people can occur, heretical
for that reason; in that that specificity is the *world* (CP, "The Provi-
dence," p. 415) unraveled from 'that' mind imposition.

It is ahead of the dissolution of the self as 'real.'

The form of the *Collected* can be a being in 'history' by virtue of its
ground/the individual poem (that is, the particular configuration/form of
a conflict as a component in a series of such) *not* mirroring that which is
outside. It is to be the opening of a space (that of American "doing noth-
ing") which is what is really outside—that is, outside of the mind's con-
tinual imposition of their/its own form. Resisting one's/and *their* (CP,
"They," p. 417) 'formation' I think is the meaning of Creeley's comment:

I've always been embarrassed for a so-called larger view. I've been given to write
about that which has the most intimate presence for me . . . I think, for myself at
least, the world is most evident and most intense in those relationships. Therefore
they are the materials out of which my work is made. (*Contexts*, p. 97)

Creeley's use of autobiographical reference is following the movement of itself in time (watching the mind)—rather than the expression of 'creation' of a personality. Its mirroring of its own mind formation and its race to outrun that as 'serial thinking' is not static personality creation *because* it is only that movement.

This internally produced 'argument' (the mind watching itself and trying to outrace its own closure, as a 'particular' form in this time) rather than being a trap that ultimately enshrines the self, are pieces in the collection of writing that by the very fact of occurring as 'merely' components repeating a conflict, as it shows up, *without* essential change, are not 'that' (fixed) psychology.

The central fear of the 'Puritan ethos' is that which is 'internally produced'—heretical precisely because it is the American "doing nothing," what Creeley identifies in Williams: "He knew that you change your mind every time you see something, and—what is it he says?—'A new world is only a new mind.' So the context is continually what you can feel and where you are" (*Contexts*, p. 17).

An example of traditional orientation: placing writing that is phenomenological in categories such as "lyrical" "expressivity" "imagination" (categories meaning 'individual' 'personal' only)—is 'to remove' it from its gesture.

(At the same time) the grounds for elimination of eroticism in say Marxist poetics (see "The Cannon") is that eroticism is 'private'/personal. As in traditional social convention, the erotic is the area quintessentially subjective and egoistic; the poetic-political argument being even that eroticism itself is inherently sexist. That's what *social context* does reflect.

If eroticism is suppressed (socially or in poetics) in the sense of our not seeing it in or as being the occurrence, that leaves only that social context (which is defining or determining); there is then no area existing for apprehension, or change.

One has to write 'on' 'subjectivity'—as that being without entity: as such, contentless—*by being* subjectivity (by having only that ground; and by that being seen to be "subjectivity" as a socially devalued characteristic *per se*). By being 'not' is—(contentless).

For example, eroticism as writing constructed to be that as genre could be contentless as being *outside* the 'social'—that it is *not* given high value. In other words, erotic is socially *defined* as 'outside'/as 'personal' (in the convention that I'm terming 'American ethos': so *there* it 'can be' contentless but only negatively as lust without relation to other, that is, as sexism). In order to *be* 'outside,' eroticism would have to be *there* as 'that'/'eroticism' only, a double that is "doing nothing."

Therefore one could make a ground of eroticism 'only'—not as "obsession" or reaction but a gesture observing itself, therefore 'contentless.'

An example of this idea in my own writing: *Instead of an Animal* is a serial poem that is substitution—by 'only' sexual behavior being there (substitution of children for adults, or adults for 'animals,' or 'animals' for unknowns as if implied blanks in the text—like musical chairs). Interpretation of the series 'in terms of' its content belies it. It does not reflect psychology. It's 'the opposite' of obsession by repeating. As serial, it both is and isn't what its subject is—so it's outside of that as definition (starting with being outside its own 'definition' as its shape/in simple repetition, which as such is change). In other words, the serial is outside of being 'on' sexual gestures only *or* 'being contentless,' either.

'The real actions of/in the world,' what we experience as real, with oneself together,[3] is seen as merely the self, which, when the *world* allows only itself, isn't of the 'real.' Creeley's saying self is only being the 'real.'

Robert Wilson's form of theater presentation is many scenes unfolding beside or out of each other, which therefore seemingly take place within a limitless context. The quality of its not being in a 'box' derives from its emanating from the viewer; the action is the viewer's seeing it. Similarly, Creeley's *Collected* has the quality that 'you' are creating it.

The fact that Wilson's visual spectacle unfolds unmediated by language (in the unfolding seemingly not being formed by language—our impression is not 'informed' by it) creates a sense of sites/sights essentially not changed from their 'original.'

The viewer is seeing the unfolding scenes and ordering them as a 'history.' Creeley's *Collected* maintains its 'original seeing,' repeating it as oneself seeing it.

The conflict delineated in *For Love*, *Words*, and *Pieces* of one being precisely the same as one's opposite/of 'other' (such as 'Creeley' being *the same as* 'woman'/mother: in the measure of the poem, being that configuration)—therefore nothing in oneself—and the relation to that duo being separation *per se*: is an enactment continually of split that is its gesture only. It's just that.

The gesture of Creeley's *Collected* (viewed as itself a series) being 'it's noting chronology' itself—is an 'American' tracing of "nothing," which is being 'what really is.' 'Where?'

Notes

A version of "'Thinking Serially' in *For Love, Words*, and *Pieces*" was published in Leslie Scalapino's *Objects in the Terrifying Tense/Longing from Taking Place* (New York: Roof Books, 1993); and *Disembodied Poetics: Annals of the Jack Kerouac School*, ed. Anne Waldman and Andrew Schelling (Albuquerque: University of New Mexico Press, 1994).

1. Robert Creeley, *The Collected Poems of Robert Creeley, 1945–1975* (Berkeley: University of California Press, 1982), p. 437. Cited hereafter in text as "CP."
2. Robert Creeley, *Contexts of Poetry: Interviews 1961–1971* (Bolinas, Calif.: Four Seasons Foundation 1973), p. 101. Cited hereafter in text as *"Contexts."*
3. "One would be destroyed by the writing being that of only those 'actions in the world,' no other existing. The converse is to allow for the small self in continual imbalance: in which the 'world' is part of and 'within' the defenseless self.

"H.D. allows the imbalance: a sense of an infinite structure of possible actions that is in the world overwhelming the tiny self: is the *form* of the writing." (From Leslie Scalapino, "An H.D. Book" in *Objects in the Terrifying Tense/Longing from Taking Place*. New York: Roof Books, 1993.)

:: *The Recovery of the Public World*

To get to the relation to the public—by recognition of absence, of no relation—to the other

Description 'before' event is hierarchical structure—of (is/as) values; so that the "event" does not take place, at all. A dismantling of perception—so that hierarchical structure is not that perceiving—changes occurrence itself.

Essay on Nāgārjuna (who lived approximately one hundred years after Christ; his thought is regarded as a foundation of Zen): Nāgārjuna's *Seventy Stanzas* are a logic of phenomenal emptiness. A phenomenon can't be 'arising,' since in order for it to be in existence it has to have 'arisen' already—which it can't do in or from itself either; so it isn't inherent, hasn't independent existence. It can't have ceased (as it hasn't arisen nor is there: as there's no moment of its occurrence). It can't *be* ceasing—as *it* is not entity, nor has it been caused.

A phenomenon hasn't inherent existence—as it is not based on a single moment of a mind, nor on successive moments of a mind, as such moments arise dependently (don't exist inherently, not being that phenomenon itself—though appearing to be). In other words, the apprehension or the 'moment' of the mind appears to be the phenomenon itself, which the mind itself is seeing. Neither exists inherently.

Ignorance cannot originate as a cause, except in dependence on chains of phenomenal formations, which themselves can't originate except in dependence on their causal connections: which is ignorance, perception itself. (They can't arise from something other than themselves, nor from themselves.)

Perception itself is phenomena.

Beginning and disintegration are devoid of inherent existence as being in perception (appearance).

For that reason, the way they appear and the way they exist are dissimilar, and they appear in a deceptive way to, and in, the world. "Like the objects of a dream they appear to have existence to ordinary perception.

So the way they exist and the way they appear are different and these conventional existences are called distortions or false."[1] *Both*, the way they exist (that is, 'fact') and the way they appear, are false.

The cause and the result of a phenomenon cannot arise with inherent existence either simultaneously or sequentially. If in one's view events' lack of inherent existence makes them completely non-existent, one cannot assert their continuity or that of the moments between them; so that view, of non-existence itself even, is inaccurate.

Poetically in present-time this suggests to me writing that is its syntactical and structural motion (doesn't exist—'there' at any place as a sole entity in the series or sequence or whole—nor in any other form than its moves) by not asserting its content simultaneously or sequentially. Authority *is* ignorance.

One is to find out what's there, *as* occurrence. Nāgārjuna's tenets do not imply even cooperation or interrelation, since interrelation is also without base.

The emptiness of the conquerors was taught in order to do away with all philosophical views. Therefore it is said that whoever makes a philosophical view out of "emptiness" is indeed lost.   —Nāgārjuna, Madhyamakaśāstra

To iterate somewhat: as no phenomena or events/constructs can be single, in that they spring from other contingencies and *are* these, they do not exist in that perceived form (single)—only appear to exist 'at present,' which also only *appears* to exist.

'Logic' is the maintenance of that appearance and set of appearances.

The deconstruction of our view of reality is oneself in one time not maintaining *either* one's own subjective view *or* the social or phenomenological interpretation of occurrences. Nor is this 'not holding a view.'

The implication of Nāgārjuna's 'logic' is the deconstruction of all logic or rationality, which (logic), as such, is not either observation *per se* or phenomena (analysis, such as that fire arises from kindling, is generalization, self-defining in laying a basis as being its own conclusion). The fire doesn't arise from kindling; fire isn't the same thing as kindling; kindling doesn't exist as fire.

Nāgārjuna's 'logic' deconstructs rationality (as that being neither observation nor phenomena) *with* observation and phenomena ('single' particularities, which have no basis in that they have no individual existence). That is, observation is deconstructed by admitting of the 'subjective,' its own lack of basis; therefore it critiques itself.

This isn't psychology or the formation of narrative based on psychology, quite the contrary. It's the dismantling of any narrative, by there being no basis—at all.

Some poetic writing at present in the United States (with various intentions and arising from various influences) articulates a critique of 'one's assumptions' (one's observation, or of perception itself as cultural) by perceiving or rendering perception as being without basis. At the same time, this examination of subjectivity in fact can work as a critique and revelation of our culture.

In other words, by undercutting the observer, one has a perspective of place that is both 'spatially' 'interior' and 'outside'—a relativity.

What must have been most threatening was the Mādhyamika's radical critique of the entire rationalist project. . . . Classical Mādhyamika authors emphatically rejected nihilistic interpretations of emptiness, although it is clear that they viewed it as the most inviting and dangerous distortion of a deconstructive critique that depended exclusively on a reductio ad absurdum for its results. Again and again they admit that the doctrine of emptiness is frightening—and *ought to be* frightening for anyone who engages with it at an emotional and volitional level through meditation—because it lends itself so easily to nihilistic interpretations. As Nāgārjuna wrote in the *Ratnāvalī* (RV, p. 26): "Beyond good and evil, profound and liberating, this [doctrine of emptiness] has not been tasted by those who fear what is entirely groundless" (p. 26).[2]

In other words, all phenomena and perception are groundless—therefore fear is groundless (as is "joy" as a state of response).

There is not a transcendent ground. The mode is not an undoing of rationality on behalf of something that transcends rationality. C. W. Huntington in *The Emptiness of Emptiness* (p. 27), comments on T. R. V. Murti's *The Central Philosophy of Buddhism*: "As Wittgenstein would say, Murti is playing an altogether different language game. Let us briefly compare his use of language with Nāgārjuna's to get a feeling for the difference between these two distinct styles of expression. Where Murti asserts that 'the real nature of things' is their 'transcendent ground,' Nāgārjuna writes: 'Everything is real (*tathyam*), not real, both real and not real, and neither real nor not real.'"

From C. Gudmunsen's *Wittgenstein and Buddhism* (New York, Macmillan, 1977) as quoted by Huntington (p. 31):

The Buddhist ultimate truth of emptiness is ineffable, then, but in a special sense—not because our words fall short of describing some transcendent reality called "emptiness," but because all words are such that they lack referential content or are "empty" of substantive meaning (*artha-śūnyaśabda*). This holds despite appearances and the common usage of words. As there are really no determinate entities to be referred to, so words do not actually refer. Their indexical function is illusory, indeed it is one of the major fabricators of illusion. What is, and the emptiness thereof, will simply not submit to the language of determinateness. On the other hand there is no other kind of language. This no doubt accounts for the intractable character of the emptiness teaching and for its frequent misinterpretation.

The intractable character of Nāgārjuna's language is that it can't be taken in any other way while holding contrary or mutually exclusive views throughout, and this can't be expressed in any other way (without *being* something else). Furthermore, what is being expressed is not determinate entities.

I'm using the example of Nāgārjuna as a way of broaching 'our' categorical conceptualization as a language of determinateness. The black-and-white categories that are tendencies of American thought approachable (in the sense of demolishing their walls) by an overtly antirationalistic mode, which as such never allows its expression to be realigned and by that integrated into category. Current poetic texts that use a logic as antirationalistic realism. The difficulty of 'reading' it becomes the process by which the reader is realigned.

One has to *seek* to be realigned.

Nāgārjuna's 'mode' as a model of 'poetic writing' implies demonstration, which is both (and mutually exclusive—at once) demonstration of thought and demonstration of action.

This implies an enjambment of states or conditions of reality. Writing that is *either* a 'lyrical expressivity' *or* convention of discourse cannot be receptive to these conditions.

Demonstration of thought alongside demonstration of action (are) on both sides (as there being that contrary) lacking in referential content.

The pressure of American perceptual convention will be to bring these into focus as contraries only, thus removing them from their dynamic relativity.

As a youth while a student at Berkeley High School, I noticed the common usage (Black or African American) of a fragment of speech functioning as a musical phrase, "Sh(a)-ma-faa" (Shit-mother-fucker); usually spoken melodiously by boys to each other, rather than spoken by girls.

The phrase had a benign, communicative use, which was exclamation of awe, or pretended exclamation of awe, which was therefore a commentary meaning the opposite; or *both* at the same time, both ironic commentary on and exclamation of awe.

It was nonreferential words, the obscenity taken into a different (not transcendent) usage by *being* that (by being obscenity). Therefore it seemed to imply being outside the 'social' as the act of creating that 'social' (communing, as two people speaking to each other only then).

By their speaking they could go past the bounds of speaking—and were also outside of any 'social' apprehension and interpretation.

Gertrude Stein's separation of "human nature" and "the human mind" is a contemplation of entity, her having the view that human nature had entity and the human mind did not; yet was still permanent. For her, impermanence is not throughout, is not entirety.

Contemporary "avant garde" (or "experimental"—but I would substitute the word "radical") practices (the practices of John Cage, Jackson MacLow, Hannah Weiner, Philip Whalen, Robert Grenier, Bernadette Mayer, Tom Raworth, Fiona Templeton, Richard Foreman, Barrett Watten, Carla Harryman, and many others [whose forms and intentions are different from each other]) can be compared to Nāgārjuna's delineation of interrelation: both the practice and perception being modes only, or operations without entity. In other words, the 'practices,' so to speak, are continually only that and also *not* that. If procedures are used, the work (text, which may also be dance, performance, video) cannot be described as inherently those procedures. Nor does 'perception' 'operate' (as the conception of that).

At the same time there is also a conservative social factor now of poets accommodating the university setting, articulating their work as "intellectual" "procedural" eschewing "experience" "avant garde." In order to be called "avant garde," the gesture would have to be devoid of its specificity *per se* (generalized, as—or as if—modes or operations without entity)—and without the practice or the perception's urgency or disturbance. Because disturbance would be entity. Yet their hierarchy is entity.

An American dancer (of "modern dance") remarked on seeing Mongolian dancers performing in the United States: "but of course that's *ethnic* dance." Thus placing it in a category disconnected from *any* vital practice.

'Not perceiving impermanence' itself becomes an action, an intention. Which enables a social separation between 'one,' as if insulated capitalist consumers (whole)—and 'other,' the rest of the world, 'experience.'

Which is 'commentary' as well.

One's constantly attempting to reintroduce 'disturbance' into the work-as-social-medium as solely an operation; because that's occurrence: in Robert Grenier's color Xerox poems as drawings enlarged and retaining the color marks (such as a band on either side of a line in the center as if horizon line) and black borders supplied by the Xerox machine, *Owl on Bough*[3]—impermanence is entirely; the words do not represent the shape of figures or phenomena.

Words shapes there as drawn (so that the words if typed would not be the same) are the only approximation of what's seen, are a form of 'direct' seeing by there being a complete separation.

The scrawled drawn catty-corner shapes as letters of "Owl" in one (right) diagonal crossing a sheet split by a center line and band around the line—"Glides" crosses the center line at the opposite (left) diagonal—the shapes and their separation in space being the motion of separation of text from itself only. Demonstration of 'no-procedure.'

([In the structure of my detective novel *Orchid Jetsam*:]'Commentary' in the form of a series of statements of intention being the actions of doing those intentions—is itself a form of 'running' in a space [that is the text] which transforms that social space, and as it were bounds into a space that is 'not subject.' Not tied to that which is social, or one's 'interior.'

"Impermanence—I wanted, in the structure throughout and in the minute unit [only one or two words on a line] as order of perception [past and present reverberating back into the 'past' of the structure at any one point at the same time

as into its future—disrupting—serene at once] occurring in the line breaks, *to have* impermanence, to seek this—positively—as a gesture in the world, outside of oneself, not 'about' one.

And that minute 'duplication' as events simply go out and out, not recurring as a prior known shape.")[4]

Robin Blaser's holy forest in the public world:

INVERSION: An interchange of position, especially of adjacent objects in a sequence.

A rearrangement of tones in which upper and lower voices are transposed, as in counterpoint, or in which each interval in a single melody is applied in the opposite direction.

> *through 'you' I conceal my loneliness from myself*
> *and make a way into the multitude and into love*
> *by lies, for my heart cannot bear the terror, and*
> *compels me to talk as if I were two5*

Blaser's is like blowing a reed instrument double on the same note.

It's a blind note that is "social, political, hellish and heavenly parts" at once. Dual as one in the form constitutes both absence and making of images, observed as making images, in order for these (the only public world) to be independent of 'me' and to be "*for* me in order to be without me":

> I make out a boat the soul's image a voice a residence
> and the disappearance from a work over the last
> blind note 'Oh, a boat of friends' the music of,
> logos of a blinding instrument our words, mine
> among them wash at the perilous social, political,
> hellish and heavenly parts

> *the world is in accordance with me*
> *perspective in order to be independent*
> *of me is for me in order to be without me*
> (p. 138)

'One,' 'you,' 'I,' sentiment, fantasy, the flesh, each is the medium rather than the language being the medium, in the sense that they are applied in the opposite direction from their language articulation while being it only ("The Medium," p. 45). The Phantoms of sentiment are other than oneself in the sense of being faculties of oneself as such: "your back is a mirror" ("Awake," p. 43).

Atlantis/known illusion lights up images of personal history as if these are held interiorly, as occurs in the newspaper. Illusion comprises the way of observing the public world only—the waves run back and "*defecate /*
to a pure transparency."

It's a logic (appearing 'as if' logos, therefore inverted only?) that is reverse-out white while still being night, so that an interior as a mental shape (indistinguishable from its language shape) is a "privacy" 'without any language' manifestation. (He's evoking two surfaces, that which can't be said—*or* be.) The logic of the language is: absence as visible illusion in which the 'you' or the 'I' sees and performs acts (as if) in the absence of language (rather than in the absence of 'I')—which effectively negates that 'I' and yields that which is the vision, the public world:

> turned by that privacy
> from such public perils as words
> are, we travel in company with the messenger . . .
>
> . . . (in the moonlight
> white blossoms hastening to fall
> are cut free)
>
> then we, the apparatus, burned by a night
> light, are travelling in company with the messenger
> ("Image-Nation 2 (roaming," p. 62)

The 'I' acts apart and *is* the other (while the other is its own self, by definition): "naked, an unyielding form of I acting apart, / but it is Naught the other is that unlearned."

> further out as the eyes of the cat
>   if she would be
> free from words, she would free me even in the night
>
> there are birds summoned by words
>   (P. 100)

Birds and words are separate and are in utter pleasure; and 'I' and words are separate; as 'I'/objects/phenomena and language are "full of invisible motion / shaped out of their origin." The messenger is the compression.

Blaser's poetic lines are minute absences compressed (illuminated by and as this compression, as movement), which is the realistic world:

> many times one falls out of the mortal
> there suddenly the missing outward
> journey
>
> o we do *in all things*
> *walk contrary to the world*
>   (P. 113)

The translation of oneself into the other is the movement and shape of its language only. The images of the war are like or 'as if' language rather than the reverse. Words, as the compression of the absences, do not add to the real but rather compose it. In the future. The blind note and the heavenly are therefore interchangeable.

> like small poems read from
> vast stages the images of the war
> in Vietnam burn up out of the
> words,
>   where they are not
> added to the real
> but compose it
>   (P. 114)

Meeting on the Line, Sphericity: In Mei-mei Berssenbrugge's writing, change can sweep across the whole structure, is even retroactive.

In *Sphericity*,[6] which is a collaboration with artist Richard Tuttle, when a point is silent, it's not a vantage point. Really there's no vantage point, and the instant of apprehension *is* solely. The event horizon is so loaded, the horizon's everywhere: "the seam, my experience of your experience, a horizon at dawn, is the instant of apprehension."

Where everything changes, where there is no vantage point or sound in writing, "she couldn't say the experience or absence is changing"—nor is such a point existence *per se*.

The content of phenomena is scrutiny, according to Berssenbrugge. Her comparison of objects, qualities as events is on a line (of her scrutiny) compared to 'some other's' "event horizon," their line where events occur. The two lines are collaboration between Berssenbrugge and Tuttle here.

There is no stability of the structure (of the poem or visual aspect) except the line of occurrence, which is 'their' apprehension.

The criteria are that an event is subject to its scrutiny only. Its apprehension *per se* is an event. In that sense there are no comparisons.

Berssenbrugge subjects 'seeing' an event to language. Berssenbrugge's writing is drawing relations continually, on a hypothesis that writing is *other* than, a different faculty from, vision. *Sphericity* subjects the comparison itself (Tuttle's seeing/perspective and Berssenbrugge's language) to *comparison*. The 'comparison itself' is Berssenbrugge's long line of the poems, which, as a measure/shape that extends throughout the text, is as if there were one infinite line of 'relation' that constitutes the "event horizon" of *Sphericity*.

That line as such is also an 'illusion'; spheres seen only by their exten-
sion on a plain that can't be seen.

'Nature' is seen, in Berssenbrugge's writing, by its being at the line of
its occurring (as writing). There 'it' is only 'relations' to other phenom-
ena, where 'nature' and the object are occurring from being/absent.

Tuttle's faintly drawn words (as if imitating or reflecting words of
Berssenbrugge's that are on the page opposite) are drawn beside or
nearby his minimal graphic shapes, the words at the bottom or side on a
page, a sense of their being absent in the middle (a sense of absence is
produced by his shapes being in relation to a middle—which is also con-
ceived in relation to two facing pages). "The plane of yourself separates
from the plane between objects" by the space of Tuttle's shapes and of
Berssenbrugge's words. There is therefore no logos (cosmic reason). (It's
not relying on connections, but these being there.)

Comparisons extinguished on the line (horizon) are peaceful and
'goalless' there.

Notes

Part of *The Recovery of the Public World* was given as a talk for the 70th Birth-
day Celebration of that title for Robin Blaser in Vancouver, Canada, 1994.

1. David Ross Komito, translated by Geshé Sonam Rinchen and Tenzin Dor-
jee, *"Nāgārjuna's Seventy Stanzas,"* A Buddhist Psychology of Emptiness (Ithaca,
N.Y.: Snow Lion, 1987), 82.

2. C. W. Huntington, Jr., and Geshé Namgyal Wangchen, *The Emptiness of
Emptiness, an Introduction to Early Indian Mādhyamika* (Honolulu: University
of Hawai'i Press, 1989).

3. Robert Grenier, *Owl On Bough* (Sausalito, Calif.: Post-Apollo Press,
1998).

4. Leslie Scalapino, *Orchid Jetsam*, manuscript.

5. Robin Blaser, *The Holy Forest* (Toronto: Coach House Press, 1993), 139.
Hereafter cited in text by poem title and/or page number only.

6. Mei-mei Berssenbrugge, drawings by Richard Tuttle, *Sphericity* (Berkeley,
Calif.: Kelsey St. Press, 1993).

As: All Occurrence in Structure, Unseen

:: *The Weatherman Turns Himself In*

For Zack

Note: *Deer Night* is rendition of: 'one'-as-interior-of-'here'-and-'Asia.'
The Weatherman Turns Himself In is: rendition of 'this' location 'only.'
Both are modes of 'excluded articulation.'

The Weatherman is 'demonstration as action' which is at once commentary as interior; one 'to be' only outside there. It is the 'appropriation' of one's own gestures, gutting them so there is only luminous actions in light. Interior/private, as the viewer, is 'demonstration of action.' Because the commentary 'could' only be its occurrence 'at the same time.'

One's mind is always a 'prior' or 'later' action. The intention here is one's mind (either speaker or viewer) being aware of being separate cognizing—as one's simultaneously doing (which is also cognizing) an action or motion. The 'two' are together 'then.'

This is also a demonstration of the conception of 'play' as 'simultaneously silently read text' (see "Silence and Sound/Text" and "Footnoting"). 'The two, as action and reading, being together' are only silent, can't be pronounced. The "Notes" (such as this one) function as integration, interrelation, and 'introduction throughout.'

The poem-play is form of discourse as 'public experience,' trying to create the communal: the designated parts are not characters, but rather 'interior' conversation ('seeing' one's own thought), speaking outside and viewing inside. Viewing text itself. As if one's mind is at once an other limb's physical motion.

CHARACTERS

Eyes-lowered, a woman with ascetic appearance of mercenary saint, almost shaved head, wears white dress
The Other, a sprightly woman, wears black dress
The Weatherman, a man, wears white suit, has black paint on his eyes on white face.
News-people, a man ghoul, as news media, with slab of yellow teeth which he puts in for action scenes when he's not speaking; wears white

suit. He becomes other people: unknown motorcyclist who attacks Eyes-lowered; also the illuminated dog; and a waiter at the cafe.
An Outsider, man, wears white suit.

All have white paste or powder on their faces. An ocean of sewn black silk irises (flowers) attached on strings hangs from the ceiling in the field (location) where the audience sits.

Flowers are eyes. The viewers are compressed into state of illusion—seeing there is no illusion—in the surface.

SCENE 1

Each of the speakers is speaking 'out of' a separate locale/scene all occurring at the same time. They, the individuals and scenes, do not refer to each other. They're absorbed in their own spheres. Weatherman is standing in a tub of water (blue shiny flecks of paper). The play uses the spatial terrain of white background, and the blackness of the ocean of hanging black irises (where the audience is). All of the other actors are lying on the floor as if dead as the audience comes in, except the Outsider who sits motionless on the top of a ladder.

WEATHERMAN: The black ocean of irises is hanging in a half sky.

Not even jetting on the black stream, as that is an image of one (or of oneself)—not have an illusion.
There too, rebelling—in the illusion one is in.

OUTSIDER (*sits on the top of a ladder*): Conceptualization is dead scenes, as is the ocean of black irises open not reflected anywhere—so it was born. This is not therapy, which is *our* sense here of a goal (that would be individuals being for a reason, to be cured), yet landscape has no determination before—?
There are only people starving and running—and can throw the bar—the helpless blue itself. Seeing.

WEATHERMAN: They robbed banks and shot one, the Weathermen of the terrorist group, later by the ocean of irises non-reflecting.

Not seeing it (the ocean of irises)

OUTSIDER (*gets down from ladder*): This is ordered only chronologically. (*He crouches unraveling a cord, so that it is the line on the floor separating the audience from the actors.*) The line is by the ocean of irises non-reflecting. It's seen to be nothing. It's visible only on the line.

WEATHERMAN: What did you do while you were away? Is anything away? I moved toward the iris and coupled with a deer.
    I walked to the iris in the day. Where is the iris in the day?
    There's no motion in the day by itself.

EYES-LOWERED: They define "gregarious" as only itself, cattle pushing, as the quality of the social person, that *being* a person as such. Otherwise the person is nothing. Whereas, rebelling is the obverse, refusing the illusion—the only way in which one can be.
    This—rebelling—is the sensitive nature I do not possess, though it is there, like moving through fields that are before one.

OUTSIDER: Doesn't love *them*—not *there*. Rather the illusion for them is of the black stream itself, so that a creature passing in front of it on it could be seen—to be seen on the stream jetting on it as oneself.
    Doesn't reflect one if not reflecting themselves.

WEATHERMAN: The people seen nearby the voluptuous hanging lips of the black irises that are hanging on the stream of night—the people and the irises don't arise from night.
    People swim through heavy water trying to arise to the black which is the other's sky.

OTHER: Breath night. The lips of the irises breathe.

EYES-LOWERED: Breathing in accelerated thin black flowers.

OTHER: This friend came; she said that I didn't love people as I didn't see my view as inferior to theirs when I was small, the seed of seeing my view. My view not being inferior, that not existing—*isn't* in an illusion? No, I have to *not* exist as being in conflict, *then*.
    —sites in (written space) of erotica, which by being only their own

minute movement, as only *their* phenomena, are delight—simply (flimsy, 'feminine,' therefore not regarded by critical theory, as such undercutting as simply outside of authority—there too, rebelling).

The juxtaposition, and the removal of juxtaposition even, of images or movements, changes reality, which is perception.

Anecdotal is not trusted as thought, as objective observation? Place pressure on the minute anecdotal so there appears to be *only* such.

WEATHERMAN (*addressing no one standing in the tub, pointing*): A burly orange cat running in the rain, its coat holding so much water heavy barrel pulling it down—tries to outrun its burly orange coat, for it.

Why do you have no confidence? Why do you have confidence?

OUTSIDER (*still as it were listening to the Other*): Having learned to breathe as accelerated motion at all times, in her upper chest only, as if running always, even when not moving—her other lower chambers are frozen; they can be reawakened only without the condition of sprinting while quiet, and breathing in them.—But she wants to be actually sprinting and quiet, breathing in the deeper chamber and as if calmly not moving.

> The Iris of the Deer
> On the Red Sea, the irises are blooming in red.
> The irises standing in waves, one emerges through the iris.

As if the *visible* not reflecting occurs, only.

SCENE 2

OTHER (*lying down on floor and peeling tangerines*): I lay having a sense of jeering and the man's held out to me who's died now having been thin gentle teaches me to bow had been in drag at some time is out on the field doing nothing. Floating. They just do that.

Living for days on a bag of tangerines I bought when I skittered back. Don't even sit up in bed just reading not coming out. This is being a hermit. (*Outsider makes a grunt as if making fun of her. As if answering him:*) It isn't interior value.

OUTSIDER (*he's referring to The Other's relation to Eyes-lowered, who's sitting as beatific head-lowered posture*): The (Other) is brought into her presence, who wants the other to do a job and is controlling in a passive-aggressive manner by keeping her eyes down so that one would have to get on the floor lower to speak. She is cadaverous, doesn't speak. They are out at a party surrounded by people.
(*News-people is lying on the floor, is brought forward by the Outsider to participate with the Other and Outsider as they mime speaking at the party.*)

EYES-LOWERED (*The Other leaves the platform, is brought to Eyes-lowered by Outsider. Eyes-lowered speaks of herself*): There isn't interior to it as it's filled with animosity sporadically or continually. The other is to protect it. People do come and sit beneath it speaking.

OTHER (*she has knelt looking up into the face of Eyes-lowered*): The Other who has the job of protecting her responds with animosity as the Outsider from not being liked. The cadaver would not give off a perfume, not speaking. One might as well lie in the gutter like the dog as one just lives.

OUTSIDER (*as if about himself and in reference to Eyes-lowered*): Somehow the information about the job is communicated by someone who appears to be her husband, standing at her side. She may be deaf. Her nostrils quiver.

OTHER: The cadaver makes a very hard-boiled remark about not having time to do this work.
    The (other) feels giddy and happy as she just lives.

SCENE 3

OTHER (*sits on the ladder looking down on the others*): In the thin clear morning, a group is talking conviviality saying they'd just figured out that we'd end (they're in the middle) but it's not so bad until then.
    They mean dying as ordinary and so it's atonal.

(*Eyes-lowered makes expansive motions of walking slow in bright blue light landscape. Light bounding, it is the walk of a predatory creature 'on the run' sweeping through.*)

OUTSIDER: Out on the Boulevard Saint Sebastopol when the early morning is very thin and light past a newspaper stand. The water from the bridge is reflected by the slight rungs of clouds in the early sky. A dove flies by in the thin air.

The saint past the walking figure in a taxi not seeing. Her lips are pressed, seen sideways, the eyes now not lowered but very piercing. The taxi stops at the bank.

(*Light up on News-people rolling by himself on floor being illuminated dog appearing to be whipped*)

The cadaver emerging as if from the crypt of the bank into the light. Holds a valise in her thin hand. Some fundamentalists are beating the illuminated dog, to one side. Bending over it with whips, with the dog's side open and trailing the entrails.

Pause while the Other contemplates sky. News-people exits.

OTHER: The bat is almost not born, not being at dusk. One bowing is that. It's being in the blue day, not at night; it's not being on the red where it's flying.

Eyes-lowered slips and falls slowly, moves as if trying to rise and groping kneeling, her neck swaying in the movement as if she's being swept. News-people wearing motorcycle jacket and carrying helmet is yellow-toothed rider swirling slowly drawn-out as if being thrown. His neck thrashes, mouth open. The Other is running as slowed drawn-out movement hitting the 'cycles' not visible that arch in the air; the Other may use a cloth bar which when she throws it makes no sound, or a metal bar. Sound track of motorbikes or actors make that sound.

OUTSIDER: Eyes-lowered steps into the street, facing away from them. As if deaf, though the sound is ordinary of motorbike which meets her. She's lying kneeling. The fume of the motorbike in the air.

She's lying in the gutter without the valise floating. The (other) had been running.

NEWS-PEOPLE (*referring to Eyes-lowered*): Was past it, which was kneeling. Groping. With space around it, and then cars moving swirl over it.

OTHER (*referring to herself, and running on the others toward Eyes-lowered*): As from not being liked and so without there being anything runs.

OUTSIDER: Hitting the tin tail of the motorbike. So that the yellow-toothed rider whips his neck glinting skids.

NEWS-PEOPLE: (*speaks standing when movement has receded*): Yellow-toothed rider is right on her, the bike whirring to one side. His neck thrashing.
    Then goes back to bike and starts it and rides off.

EYES-LOWERED (*uttered in gutteral manner, referring to herself*): The shrouded eyes, balls hovering, the lids hang on them. The lids flutter on them obsequiously.
    Will flutter obsequiously on her bearers, as they're flickering carrying her some time.

OTHER: Her not seeing anyone in the stream, I'm working for her and turn and follow to see the blind ocean around; in whose mass as she's hurrying forward clutching the suitcase, her gel eyes in which a nerve may be seen floating,

NEWS-PEOPLE (*all are clustered around Eyes-lowered*): a clot in the center like a jellyfish mass, a colony, do not reflect.

OTHER: She never takes drugs or food. No cell is addicted, or the clot at the center usually registering any changes faintly,

OUTSIDER (*looks up*): a cloud not mirroring the light city crossed by the long street thrown at dawn.

OTHER: The street is thrown in light at dawn, where one rolls in the light. As if in the rolls (air) of light dawn.

Eyes-lowered reenacts her slow fall, her neck swaying while she's kneeling.
OUTSIDER: Eyes-lowered that when the lids open but are concealing are packs hardened gel with the clot faintly or not registering apparently is thrown at dawn.

OTHER: The other who's hired merely a seeing-eye dog but way behind in the wake rolls walking in the wave that's dawn.

OUTSIDER: Eyes-lowered opening them don't mirror individually the vast traffic where motorcycles have bobbed up on the light above the sheet of cars. Hovering, then subsiding, reentering falling into the mass of traffic again. The (other) entering throwing bar; from far away, as she sees those in a stream approach. Eyes-lowered, tin bike glances tips up above the light reflected from the sheet of hoods.

OTHER: She throws a bar into the arch of a cycle rising floating which subsides.
(*She throws the bar into stillness*)

SCENE 4

News-people moves in tail-end of arching motion as if he's been hit in the middle and flies. Then he speaks when motion is ended.
NEWS-PEOPLE: The (other) is a bruised guard. Cycle glances off of her twisting so *they're* in the blue air. (The rider also is in the blue air.)

She has a thought.

OTHER: The blue does not reflect. They float in it. It is reflec*ted*.
The viewer is not in action.
There's a deep ocean that's black in action. (In blackened air as it's not seen.) Not seen, and don't arise in it, move from the place of action into it. Silver images are not of objects, merge not reflecting. When the images are in the ocean they're not seen by the viewer who's there. Pink tulips are the ocean open under the moon. The viewers are amidst the tulips in the black.

SCENE 5

OUTSIDER: The Weatherman in turning himself in does not give up his ideals, though surrounded by the fins in the airless crowd.

WEATHERMAN (*standing in pool of water*): The fins in the stream are news-people as silent. Their gloating emerges from their mouths but their existence, a fin in existence, is separate from any sound.

The crowd is white in the black edge of air. There's a corpse rotting in the white air, air that (we) see as only blackened.

The Weatherman turns himself in. There's not a fin near him, though they're gloating in the white air. Which can't be seen.

OUTSIDER: Bechtel now rules where there'll be no unions. The Weatherman had been on the run and in hiding for twenty-four years, now given himself up. He had hit a policeman. The moon doesn't reflect anything and is much nearer to us (than what? than anything). This is action, where everything doesn't reflect (only).

WEATHERMAN: So one's in darkness the huge light sky.

SCENE 6

NEWS-PEOPLE *as he enters in floating slow movements. His body makes motions slightly suggesting hyena's torquing of muzzle thrusting.*

They were gloating. One floated teeth bared up to a raft taking immigrants in the fired air. They watched them lie. They'd be weeping slaves. A bat on the water has no moon. Its only motion is on the water, not reflected in it.

The pale moon ball as social rebellion doesn't float. It floats.

Bechtel's the moon. It floats.

OTHER *observing News-people, the first time of connecting with him*: Children, so they are not reflecting, have no labor unions. The moon that runs pale ball doesn't float. The pale moon doesn't reflect the ocean of irises under it open, they are the ocean.

OUTSIDER: Eyes-lowered makes certain minute moves only, in her life, until one sees those certain moves and all gestures even have no connection to the outside, to reason. Whoopi.

There's no reason and this is the mere indication.

NEWS-PEOPLE: The press running and then the legs shaking while the muzzles pulled at people who'd fallen.

The gloating anchorwoman asks in the crowd. . . .

OTHER *as if the anchorwoman coyly*: Did you want to speak to me?

OUTSIDER (*The Outsider is pulling a rubber strand of 'wieners' from the coat of News-people who's lying on the floor*): The hind legs shaking while the twisting torque of the muzzle fastens and pulls the wieners from one, running with it.

NEWS-PEOPLE: One drags a purple wiener strand from a person and runs to a cobalt cloud on the field.
That was me.

OUTSIDER: That was me.

NEWS-PEOPLE: We can *only* be happy. (only)
as there's no reflection. That's what bliss *is*.
If the huge sky doesn't reflect, one bows.
They all begin bowing, bobbing like corks sporadically in different spots, as if the performance is over.

SCENE 7

OTHER *as News-people slowly makes motion as if beginning to float into air separating from bike*: She hurls a bar, her thighs curled on her sides floating in the air, then falling; the bike bar-in-wheel twists away in the blue falling.

OUTSIDER: Thighs curled on one's sides, one rises on the bike above the sheet of cars. One springs from the bike thrown in the blue.

Floating movements as the Other, News-people, and Outsider converge, merge, come apart as if moving on the street.
OTHER: The other is far away in the hurling bikes where they come in further on slashing at Eyes-lowered who's concealing hurrying carrying the suitcase.

NEWS-PEOPLE (*he's now hanging upside-down in the rungs of the ladder wearing his motorcycle helmet and jacket*): One's thrown in dawn.

Hung heads-down there are no words. Do words float up as the moon's coming down bouncing even with the red ball's line. Where's speaking in relation to the line of the moon's confidence bobbing?

Wave of crowd as we're bombing other's marching lines, the news pandering decimating, the gloating anchorwoman asks in the crowd. . . .

OTHER: Did you want to speak to me?

NEWS-PEOPLE: to them in the crowd.
(*He says with enthusiasm:*). . . . . a double canned whammy(!): to be canned twice, and yet to be a ghoul really.

As the realistic being dead while living and ridiculing the living—and to be the news-people.

OTHER: There must have been a time. A lens in light can look at past events which though no longer occurring can still be seen. A faint imprint of a past event still exists and can be seen.

WEATHERMAN *in a locale that is not in reference to the others*: The Weatherman turns himself in. A man stopping one walking crossing in the middle of the street asking for money for his car though his car's moving, one gives him ten. If he wants to con one, here. You want to con me, here.
Weatherman holds out money. News-people in floating movement as if being hit, the face floating back in the air, yellow teeth seen, is enacted at the same time as Outsider is speaking.

OUTSIDER: The news-people gloating ghouls come up. One yellow teeth cemented in a rack of yellow floating back in the pale flesh (of the face), as he is hit by a policeman, chopped in air retreats somewhat.

He retreats at the edge of the air. Then re-emerges the yellow rack shimmers in white air, in which the crowd emerges.
They all surge forward in a line like ghouls toward the audience, the yellow teeth of News-people bared, until they're eliminated by darkness.

SCENE 8

Scene continues Scene 7 with no separation. Sense of action/locales continuing without ceasing. Music taken from quick scenes from cartoons was interspersed in the production.

WEATHERMAN *speaking in separate locale from others. The Weather-man's manner is always deadpan. He is taking pictures with a camera, then laying photos of the actors on the floor even with the cord that is 'the line' of action*: The viewer is not reflected in the iris. The silver precipitates as black, the object (now the viewer) is seen only negatively, not being (there).

The viewer sees one, who is the object now, non-reflecting as being from the ocean (as of irises. The viewer is there); yet the ocean is *them*, not being reflected to one (who's them). One is not *live*, as the moon isn't, which doesn't reflect the ocean of irises open under it.
(*Stands after laying the photos and gives an explanation:*)

The viewers, who are among the black irises, see a horizontal plain of distraction. The viewers are only quiet.

They are attentive only after a while.

The action in the horizontal landscape is a distraction.

Throwing a bar, with one's legs curled flying in the blue, is the Other. The viewers see this.

Yet they are quiet. There is no inner. The condition they're in is that, of no inner.

EYES-LOWERED: One is born at the edge of blackened air.
lowers eyes, lashes flutter, voice is guttural, she's speaking to herself and moving on the 'line' between the audience and space of actors: One could have no structure *and* be petulant. In the moment of one's dying no structure—*and* have the view one is to be taken care of.

OTHER: The landscape (the sense of horizontal, multiple scenes taking place, in even a really insular setting) and the occurrence of the past impinging and being in the present are curiously the mind in a state of rest. It is 'provoked' into being still and calm from making its own strain apparent even bathetic. Social rebellion creates that.

OUTSIDER: The ocean is resting, where everyone is; action doesn't originate in the non-reflecting ocean, which is not producing, the moon running above in it not reflecting it.

Muscle weighing only in the black air. Everyone is starving and running. You are defensively arguing.

OTHER *sarcastically*: Action occurs in this ocean but doesn't arise from it.

Spectacle floats location.
(*Repeats with wonder:*) Spectacle floats location.

OUTSIDER: Mind (in the viewers) causes separation of the place and white eyelids carried. It causes separation of one's inner and the real place where it's occurring.

The visible construction of landscape inseparable from action, seeing as apparent memories but occurring only as speaking, is the 'viewer' observing only one's present mind.
Landscape is event, as if one's action were seen outside one.

(*He walks into audience which is in darkness:*) The viewer doesn't have the illusion of creating action. There isn't any illusion; because the action's being produced outside of its field which is the black ocean of unborn irises.
(*Meaning the stage:*) We can see a movement as it occurs outside but it comes from only *there*. (From where it is, i.e. outside of the ocean.)
It's still and isolated, slow by being alone in life.

OTHER: Non-hierarchical form as a structure of thought is not going to be 'valued' generally, precisely because it is not normative. In a work of thought, rather than attached to a frame, one would have to have only thought as action to have no hierarchy.

OUTSIDE: One's saying that when there, where the action (one's in) is arising.
That would be at the line of black night and the blue.
Is there no movement in the unborn irises, the ocean of them?

OTHER: There's a stream of surfaces of images which apparently happen on their own.

OUTSIDER: They're not being created there, they're occurring. The 'viewer' is the individual in there, as if there were one dilated eye.

OTHER: Events are produced from (by) chronology (only)? How are they produced from being visible only. . . . ?

NEWS-PEOPLE *speaking from a locale of his own, not to others:* What's really occurring (ever) is wild so the ordinary is an imagined 'serene' basis, (or) repressed, in existence.

OUTSIDER: *This* is the illusion that past and future are contracted into the present. Yet the viewer may see that illusion itself as an implant.

OTHER: The audience may be merely distracted by the movements in front of them. The action comes from the audience—as it is compressed, it has no other (than the viewer)—but the audience is quiet and the action doesn't come from them or have any relation to them.

Lights out so there's blackness.
OUTSIDER *speaking in blackness*: The white waves of the night sky make an ocean of night, which doesn't reflect the ocean of irises below it. The irises that are not born are there, not reflecting the night sky.

WEATHERMAN *calls, holding up the tub in front of himself as if offering it to the audience*: Our refrigerator is your oyster. Floating in the blue.

The Weatherman, who wears a trench coat and fedora, pours the tub of sparkling blue flecks over his head

SCENE 9

Eyes-lowered, Outsider, and Weatherman hold onto imaginary subway train straps gently swaying to motion of moving train. News-people begins to come through train in slow motion, the Other a ways behind him 'in aisle of train' swaying as if slowed unable to get to him.

EYES-LOWERED: A short sight is not interrupted. A long sight is not interrupted. There is not an illusion.

OTHER: Train passing through the air as pearl waves her head floating in it, they who'd been on the boulevard after her come into the car hardly moving the fin.

WEATHERMAN: The fin barely moves as they go through the car face down swinging. The heads hanging yellow teeth float in an open mouth.

OUTSIDER: The head almost floats on the ocean (of pearl air)

The occurrence of sleep in the living isn't from day and night.

I sleep in the day. Is sleeping a reflection in day? Yet, lashes flickering head sunken so that is an employee who has to get down kneeling under the head lowered passive-aggressively isn't sleeping. Is day a reflection at all?

OTHER *speaks sarcastically about Eyes-lowered, as if internally, not in response to Outsider*: She's existed in night or day with no dreams occurring in either.
    She's running with the suitcase and the figure pushed yellow teeth wavering on bulb that's the sun sinking on sky within the crashing train.

WEATHERMAN: The other passengers on the flicking train sitting bob in the wavering hot bulb of the sun within the train.

EYES-LOWERED: Fin comes out toward her adrift in the train car the yellow teeth bobbing on it. The neck swings as he's making his way to her where she's holding the straps swaying in the car. Her eyes are piercing under the quivering lids. He unfolds his arm to bar her, the sun ball swimming on the line. She cuts him on the belly with a knife as he reaches her on his hand. Her lids are over the eyes which are only white in the ocean of grass through which the train plows.

As Eyes-lowered is speaking, News-people is floating toward her as if running through the car but in slow motion; she turns to face him as she's holding the train strap swaying, his arm floats out as if to bar her, and she stabs him. The Other is further back in the car, behind him, as if not able to float to where they are in time, as she is to protect Eyes-lowered. The Other's face makes gyrations as if stills of fear or horror as Eyes-lowered stabs him. Eyes-lowered exits.

OUTSIDER: Then the train reenters the roofs flicking by.

THE OTHER *speaks as now inside the memory of a different time and circumstance, no longer in the train which has faded in existence*: Bounding, so the twisting motorcycle falls in the blue—I'd thrown a bar in. Someone. . . . a person. . . . is in danger yet one is asleep inside.
    When lying on the bed, one rises on the rib cage not on the legs. One throws a bar in the wheels as it's in the air. Run on tin tail. One's running on the legs, yet the (one's) small rib cage of-a-bird floats in the blue.
    Swarm of bikes come in come by for a slash. He'd fallen. ahead.

When one is the middle child one has no life.

What if we remember one's events from different times of life in certain times, that everyone does this, and one is entirely different in a time with no relation to the other times?

(*They all say "hmmmm" as if considering this idea.*)

(*Sinks to her knees as the others resume formation of line of people as if in the train, swaying:*) Running on the tin tail which rises so that hit it falls in the blue. They come in for a slash on the motors and one slumped leans on one's knees. One weeps, the blade in a chamber that trembles.

OUTSIDER *speaking to no one*: A hose blew some water on me in a dream so that I moved in it which felt like wind.

WEATHERMAN *walking in some other location, no longer in the train. News-people, now the illuminated dog, with pink rubber strand of entrails from coat, rolls and writhes on the floor as if being beaten*:

I was walking on a line with the vast sun bulb as it's bobbing on the line, for it to dip below.

Some fundamentalists were beating an illuminated dog in a gutter, which backed away from them who're trying to get the entrails. It runs with the wieners trailing.

OUTSIDER (*He speaks as if translating for Eyes-lowered as she's seated on a chair making motions with her hands only, as if sign language to the Other*):

I've had so many jobs—I worked as a dishwasher—always they were jobs to be without orientation and not suited to my nature. I didn't want to become conservative, like men. The jobs were the discriminations, the lightest movement or tracks on an expanse of sand. It was grueling because after a while I couldn't make a living and the work was physically too hard for me. But I could have chosen to do something easy? The same light tracks and discrimination in something *easy* to do in which I had the bliss not even in action and in which there was equally no orientation, and was *also not my own* nature?

Motion ceases in full light.

Illuminated dog ceases movement.

OTHER *summarizing sardonically*: The viewer, who is the dark ocean or is in it, could do something easy?; in that, the running dog drags his wieners.

The running dog drags his entrails through the dark ocean then, *anyway.*

This is the negative image of life, not death but life. The running dog dragging the wieners did not learn slavery, ever.

That's when the illuminated dog is the viewer.

Motion ceases in full light

SCENE 10

OUTSIDER: Having the job of *maintaining* a person—

OTHER: Disturbed by abandonment, by someone who is not the same person (whom I'm having to maintain), (who) seen again, before me maintaining the dissimilarity of their actions to the appearance (when seen) of these actions—they do so only by *maintaining* the dissimilarity.

NEWS-PEOPLE: One looks into the face whose appearance is a mirror

EYES-LOWERED: (of *that* person only)—

NEWS-PEOPLE: void, so that the mirror of the cars ahead on the traffic is seen.

OUTSIDER: One has *failed* to 'protect' the person, *per se.* The failure to protect is disfiguration itself.

One should fail while making the urgent sincere effort, where that effort is the only motion in existence.

NEWS-PEOPLE: One's always 'hired'—

OTHER: Disfiguration is 'life' but not formed in 'one' or 'them' in the location of action or of concept (in the viewer)

yet it is occurring to the viewer.

If disfiguration is life (only), to the viewer, yet unborn, and not in the location of black ocean of irises, there's no death there either.

The black irises are in blue, exist in blue.

Action is perceived by the ocean of viewers—not *by*/from them; though who're in fact viewing, (so there's not death there).

OUTSIDER: Are they viewing in the blue?

Reproducing the passive-aggressive not-liking of the Other who has to constantly protect her who's the saint manifesting these traits—a fountain—the saint disfigures the ocean of irises. for *them*.

She exists in the blue.

NEWS-PEOPLE *hollow ghoul*: The subtext is annihilation, while the text is lyrical. It's the future.

OTHER *about News-people*: Therapy is the same as the news, ghouls pull wieners that is *explained*.

EYES-LOWERED: Here, we're cured.

Being an infant (later, when one is not), is being—from the inside?

Our 'view' is the subject here, which *is* therapy, in that it is determined and limited as such. We're to be limited to it only.

To be taken back into oneself is the wieners—the bar glancing in the blue.

OTHER: It is like infants, as if there were that, looking in the mirror and seeing only that/them, now looking and seeing only the empty streets in light with figures crawling on them, on their knees.

OUTSIDER: Someone took me to a meeting, I didn't know what the doctrine or orientation was. It was people who believed in life, not death. They had *trays* of babies lined and kept saying I'm for life, I'm not for death.

It's in one's own mind, by forgetting—(*life* is.)

NEWS-PEOPLE: The *real* future isn't a memory—? . . .

EYES-LOWERED *sarcastically*: if one's 'hired' . . .

OTHER: Giving actions those forms—is to be their double, but with no paradise at the beginning.

EYES-LOWERED: *She's down on her knees scratching in a cloud of dust*: Brooding and gesticulating—she had wakened with a bug under her helmet.

Their reality—to say that one is doing something (in the structure), as descriptive: To take the idea of doing that as being the fact of doing it.

'Now you're explaining what you're doing.'—but one isn't doing anything but outside.

OTHER: A leopard being realistically oneself having become that—as: *not* in a dream, only—meeting coming to a small pool a male antelope curled fitted into the grass. Then the antelope couples with the leopard: visual *per se* not in structure—as: all occurrence in structure, unseen.

My memory only occurs in the long past—the past going on 'long-sighted.'

Where before one was only breathing in the upper chest as if running always even when without movement—at last breathing in the motionless chamber that's deeper freeing it, though while running, it is like moving through the black irises, fields that are behind one, a gutted clear valve.

SCENE 11

The Other and Weatherman are alone; her tone throughout this scene is enthusiasm and glee. She runs straight toward him in the same straight frontal run as in her throwing the bar. Skids to a stop, then circles and runs straight to him again.

OTHER: The popular group is always mumbling counting their beads as goodies-two-shoes. They were being fostered to be followers by the old bitties, as convention which was unknown to them at the time. The others were not allowed to participate. It was arbitrary in appearance. The popular group is seen in sunlight, one riding a mutt, the illuminated dog that is at the same time as ridden being beaten by the fundamentalists. (*Weatherman gets down bowing or prostrate on the floor.*)

Bowing isn't praying, it's having nothing in relation to everything.
(*The Other puts her foot gently on the prostrate Weatherman and as if ordering him and describing her action:*)

Put my foot on you.

WEATHERMAN: *You* did then, right then.

OTHER: Running is bowing where there's no structure. Where the ante-lope play—one couples.

WEATHERMAN: The others think convention as wild. They participate: they remove structure from suffering.

Which is structure in suffering not being in memory even—suffering not being in events, because one has been in the particular motion of it.

And of utter freedom, which occurs as it—in appearance. With each other.

The man puts his part into the lips of the iris hanging in the black land.

A play (as structure) is the moment in a clear luminous action of people meeting which is being that moment—produced by what they say but unrelated, then, to that content.

This may occur by them seeming to have the same view as spoken, all of them to be the same (as if from one), yet as a view appearing to come from different locations—and not to be that content. A change realistically occurs as not known by them in advance.

SCENE 12

THE OUTSIDER (*he crosses into the space of the Other and the Weatherman and says eagerly*): Did you want to speak to me?
(*Eyes-lowered enters making motions as if shaking in the movements of the train car again. Referring to Eyes-lowered:*)
Her shoulders appear to turn in on her almost shaved head hanging, the lids or her lashes flickering on the head's hanging pendulum swaying in the burst of the train car. The sun bulb comes in as the train crosses on slats through the roofs of the city.

NEWS-PEOPLE (*looks down into the tub of 'water' that is now placed under the ladder; the others come to it leaning on the ladder gazing down as if at field that is far below them*): Flicking on the slats, at the edge a figure facing the glittering field in which here and there dark pigs float amidst lily pads, takes a dump at the edge of this view where other figures similarly merely their crouched backs release contents.

The crouched figures who are separate in the glittering green merely appear to float, a dump released from them. One at the edge, like a tube, the dump washed from the back—is not a disfiguration as sole of the field.

OUTSIDER: The sole field may be a disfiguration of itself; yet the figures are not a function of seeing them. Or that the train goes by: one time.

OTHER: A figure with the dump washing from it—hovers at the edge of seeing. There is the field.

NEWS-PEOPLE: A figure walking on the street, the sheets of rain descending, where the figures are hunched there, drops the dump washing from the back, of it—

OUTSIDER: Eyes-lowered walking with such force—(in the day, there's no force in it)—that the aged figures shake in the sheets of rain, or scamper on the street—

NEWS-PEOPLE: aged hang in a doorway taking a dump—

OTHER: Eyes-lowered's turning inward, a movement of walking with piercing eyes, is always the same in whatever location. So the simple clear location is a ripple then itself. To the outsider. . . . (*she indicates Outsider*).

OUTSIDER: Stepping into the street where the rain was falling, she was silent ahead with no expression.

EYES-LOWERED: Thunder raised the waves on a roll (of the purple clap rumpled above) in the street.

NEWS-PEOPLE: Washed figures fell away, begging, or some stranded illuminated by a flicker in the purple roll which closes again. They're lost in the dark night. To *her*. Figures shaking in the heavy descending rain. The aged take dumps on the edge, some curled in the heavy rain.

OUTSIDER *sitting sprawled at 'cafe' table*: I pity the birds, feeling that I can't deal with what they have, have to do in their reality. I fear what they have to deal with, feeling I couldn't do it.

NEWS-PEOPLE (*who is the waiter carrying a tray with drinks to cafe tables, curious*): Why? they have plenty of insects.

OUTSIDER: I didn't think in that way, (of it). I'm afraid of their/that life and death.

WEATHERMAN *seated in 'cafe' chair apart, to audience*: These (not necessarily them) are inner. Because I say so. The notion of pathos *per se* is bathos.
  Pathos is bathos . . . there's nothing we can do, an action.
  This can't be filmed because *anything* can be filmed.

SCENE 13

All are seated at cafe tables; News-people is the waiter.
OTHER *sitting sprawled at 'cafe' table*: I was sitting oiling down a vodka. It was the crack of day. Not dawn, full day. There was light everywhere. I sat outside to see it.
  I was at a cafe. Figures crouched nearby taking dumps. The water falling white and slow, a figure came up.

  To throw the bar (into the wheels that are floating in the blue)—then to gradually eliminate the ill-founded response (that is—itself—any legitimate anger or grounds for fighting and rebellion)
  and to 'have' (do) the action (of throwing the bar).

OUTSIDER *sitting sprawled at 'cafe' table as if at a different table, not 'with' her, but seeming to refer to her ironically*: Is the mind forgetting, *per se*—?

OTHER: Running on the tin tail with the bikes whirling on one in the street—is long removed from formations, of love. *Is* these long formations—not *them*.

NEWS-PEOPLE *as waiter with tray*: In the original location of formations which is one's to believe in life—when one has one's neck cut out in the clear dawn one believes that the morning is only clear. There's no flying curled form throwing a bar in it, that was on a horizon. There are no goals, or need.

OUTSIDER: Waiting for you. In the clear dawn, people coming by, there's no discrimination of the figures in light kneeling crawling.

WEATHERMAN *sprawled in 'cafe' chair a little apart from table as if at a different table. They all face and speak to the audience. They are very relaxed, laughing raising their glasses drinking and also appearing to chat silently*: The fiction one secretes is action. That's what action *is*. One—on the street—secretes it. Or it's occurring outside them.

The viewer, anyone, is the worm on the iris at night.

OUTSIDE: Waiting for you. She throws a bar in the blue. In stillness. Figures come up, killing people at cafes in light.

:: As: All Occurrence in Structure, Unseen—(Deer Night)

This is "The Tempest" for Joan Retallack and Tina Darragh

There's no difference between poem/play cycles and a single sequence that's also 'prose' now (and read in isolation). — ("we are such stuff as dreams are made on")

"Everything is spoken" — includes the directions in italics, which are also enacted; but not those in bold, which are unspoken and enacted (or suggestion of initiating action).

Setting is bundles of copper wire as red wheat field hanging in the air. Background is indigo.

(*pointing to herself*) In public, one casting aspersions to unknown one as if a deeply horrible person

the being taught 'intellect' as if it *were* something — and emotion, as if something else — isn't — is what has always been in public — here — ?

('their' [emotion and intellect] being — separate — and their being not the same as well — is hierarchy — and is seeing as it, as 'being' 'being') this is a violence to public in itself as people flocking to it.

(*They begin hurling small, soft snails as if playing ball with each other in dark blue light*)

Castigating the woman, a student coming up from the crowd of them and insulting a stranger, then goes to fawn on some other.
One of the students is a flopper, gutted, as having been flattered and made dependent is without will.

Would sunken the eyes sewn closed in the entourage?

Yet the one who is mean having been cloyed — goes to a stranger because of not knowing anything about them. Whom in dependence she insults out of the crowd, then goes to fawn on some other person.

That which is precariously seen as inner at huge brown and indigo butterfly — which occurred
is insulted by the student who comes up in the blue.

In some (others) flocking to death — wanting to get there (as contemplation in their acts —) they're qualified in contemplation itself. Even. It isn't even a rim.
They come to it. I want to have only literal vision where there is not one's eyes.

The stranger, insulted by the student, as if taken out of water cannot return with those others, who are still. This is not their evening, liquid without sun — at all, not on its rim.

thrown into the dark air — (people while running throwing snails)
the ultrasonic cries of the snails, not cries of people
at evening thousands still invading —

not invisible yet an inversion of their being and hearing them as if in ultraviolet light at dark within them (not that they were speaking) but as inversion perceived by an outside 'only.'

'Wanting to come to it' as to see death humbly — one, and crowd that ran to bow — is the string of such inverted motions 'only' (compressed, not just compared to each other); existing only as being observed — and making a gaff in one who is an outsider.

People being flattered as their liking that one (who's flattering) — seeing this is then called emotional (in single aberration, of person viewing) and is regarded as the person viewing being opposed to others — as if seen.

The destruction of experiencing *per se* is in fashion and is shallow and violent. The disjunction of their experience is hierarchy. By some other. I can't avoid it and so I do it.

The student in public asserts having seen the one's inner nature, gratu-itously.

This is a reverberation — of the separation itself — as utter. to them.

(*as if of herself*:)   To make them dependent.

Man throwing snails in darkness — *as* occurred — night itself is the mere seeing.

There is no other scrutiny. And imagined as rigor itself. There's none. It can't occur as rigor.

The man running throwing snails, and the snails that are being hurled, are qualified by night — are at night 'only.'

———————

I am making the weakest area be alone. Derision from that which is 'public' is not arising from being alone or from an 'inner' self supposedly being seen (which is how she styled it) in public and thus being castigated.

Experience isn't that weak area; one blindly have it interiorly in expe-riences.

The utterly separate — as occurred — in experience itself.

(**as he hurls snails**)   The man runs hurling snails and the darkness it-self is illuminated in light at dark. This occurred as interior present-see-ing, not memory in one.

They took photos flashing outside at my body being dumped on the table — I was in pain, saw a 'blue pool,' as I fell, as the pool was filling within my left side.

Yet I might have 'imagined' the pool forming as being blue 'correspon-ding' to their flashing with cameras outside me (I was actually seeing it inside, which is oneself? — at the same time as they're flashing — was I seeing in memory? which doesn't exist of it, formed at that instant?). The seeing was the memory.

I saw the dye throughout my left side and it went into my head. My seeing the inside of the body not with the eyes. Yet some sense on the closed eyelids as if the eyes were remembering seeing.

There can be no derision, exterior, which touches on one.

Dancer: I was running.

Meeting and the dream — in it — are separate.

One is dumped there as being the leg flecking slowly — neither intel-
lect nor emotion, theirs, none at all, and seeing — which can occur in sep-
aration (only?). Can occur backwards.
    A indigo brown butterfly not lighting — and which I saw. Not me. In
intense heat day.

*Dancer: Seeing the blue dye within myself (so not seeing on my eyes)
running.*

Physically seeing (on) one's inside, not on one's retina, but some sense
of 'it' (the inside of oneself) appearing there/on the eye in flickers,
    and the left leg flecking — in pain
    — is not in either observation occurring, nor in experience. A sensual
observing which is inherently dual itself. Neither are occurring — by/and
their being at the same time.

They cannot be accessed — cannot return.

'There' is neither — by simply bypassing existing — by observation
occurring at the same time (one is outside literally looking, seeing is more
passive, within one's own husk at dye — at the moment then — is not ob-
servation which is sole, itself)
    nor is it experience — as it is occurring

Some utter enjoyment — (and the occurrence of curiosity) — not from
there being pain — that is sole also — from existing which is sole
    only as it is not experience(d) even — there not being a contemplative
faculty or flecking — occurs as flecking even

(Flecking) is ridiculed — one's trained here (which is different from
being "taught," is more being as a pet). One's 'contemplative' faculty is
ridiculed — by one even — and the absence also of that faculty occurring
is subservient (not having arisen — or occurred — at all
    Lackeys fawning arise from pleasure, then

The leg flecking is in no suppression.

(*dryly*) Bifurcating customs — themselves — the weather is spring)

The curious even — when the leg flecking, in pain — seeing in physical nature which is not existing therefore, not even on one's retina — is not arising from pleasure or at all — hasn't social being, no experience — as such; not arising, it's not 'resuming.' (Didn't leave off — or recur) as one either

There it 'seems' to resume 'oneself' (no longer that, so no duration) — nonintentional — without impediment. As if one follows, tracks, something, resuming attention, itself.
There is no one to interrupt.
(One lay on the table, the technicians flashing.)

(That's backwards.)
In crowd — being stung as insult, one without motive, by a cattle prod; when one is not cattle. That other fawns on someone else then. The one stung had been cattle before, simply — but not now. The person coming up and stinging with the electric prod to hurt on the one who's hideless — which is as if blind flesh (not being at flesh where there are eyes is the flesh with the prod) — in excruciating pain there

(*Distinguish physical pain from the mind.* Cannot occur.)

Burning the tar at dawn on gorges — working on the roads on gorges, foreigners as the only export — living there on the road — isn't itself that life is nothing
dawn — that life is nothing
can't change one's habits which are corrosive — so that's going to be the only thing there is? Whether one is there.
enervated — habit — is not dawn — either.

Dancer: Seeing the blue dye within myself (*and therefore seeing not on my eyes*) *I was running at dawn.*

Yet the soft heavy rain was falling at the same time as clinging.

A homeless musician — having a dog that is a boxer, where he'd sit and play on the street — others fleeing return on the street by him. The dog the boxer's rear half is a tulip or pod emerging. The dog is still half existing

the pod is liquid-covered worm that is transforming the dog

The homeless musician then is not on the street. One is transformed by the pod, but appearing as oneself. The pod duplicates separately from one but close by. It isn't dreamed or dreaming. When the others at the moment pass running, the still living as that being oneselves are fleeing.

A liquid-covered worm transforming a person, who has to sleep, in daylight.

A social butterfly has no contemplative faculty (because I say so) — that is that of the other, the black butterfly seen or not able to be seen on the blue/and which is then man flying in it. There are no people but rather that faculty occurring. *In terms of plays, my gesture is 'to get to the inside of action, at any time.'*

(*she herself is the lackey*) Lackeys came up crawling to fawn on the few people who liquidated.
  "Gregarious" is the social being — in castigating — so there's relative occurrence.

(*appearing as brown indigo butterfly*)   *qualifying actions*

by being spoken

The forced collectivization occurs on red wheat fields. Perhaps forty million were liquidated in this period. People being shipped in cattle cars or shot. Or freezing as past the line itself using the line. Children straggling off the cattle cars when they are being deported. Looking for water.
  Starving children in herds are blue as if they are aliens. On the red wheat fields which don't exist — then, one wasn't born.

The brown indigo butterfly appears as man

from one not being born — is conception-making at present as the line of text as the real event

Only the wealthy supposedly were liquidated, yet those obviously destitute called "sympathisers" of the others were liquidated too.

People say about this But they were wealthy, yet themselves have far more.

one's observation solely and also one's experience solely — have no relation

The dirty canals floating garbage/shanties on stilts, people bathing — In the world people are the main exports, sold into brothels by parents; or they migrate as labor on the roads.

It isn't produced by the events *per se*. But must be its extremity, while not arising from it.

The black butterflies as the worms on the red wheat fields — irreducible as the black butterfly/which is the man flying being that. On a hot vast terrain of fields *per se*, there are no people.

I could only repeat that. It's its relation.

The relation isn't produced by suffering merely — of the real occurrence of their forced labor, the destruction of anyone *not* starving as having a food supply (seen — out — *not* swollen/distended with malnutrition are beaten), or anyone *having* enthusiasm — no emphasis is allowed in their convention.

which is that experience is not to occur.

Yet in extremity, not discounting occurrence and being that itself, the visual is an event itself.

The worm ate the red wheat field — fields are empty — on indigo night.

Hatred is. People believing in that which is conventional as occurrence/ as relative. So one cannot say it, as the occurrence is relative.

The McDonalds and Sony companies by the brothels — on the canals she's been sold at fourteen. There is therefore not an intellect that can see this as differentiated from moon (that's eliminated) and so sentiment — this is not to be 'seen' but 'giving up' (as a kind of relaxing) to be inverted in one only.

The roots ('existing' yet not there) of plants on stalks upright on stems — the wildcat, one — one would fly toward one if barred.

And it wasn't barred.

An ibex with only one horn and a red little tongue sticking out — (green bands as if tattoos on the face) — city, 'suffering emergence' seen. — But where there is no emergence — she's translucent, kneeling — because they bind them; hooves facing each other 'only' in motion.

This may be Egypt in her and she isn't there. And cattle.

(fourteen-year-olds brought in are in motion *per se.*)

(*Dancers carry Ibex on uncovered palanquin or litter. She is kneeling on her knees and on her arms which are curved backward, have hooves on them like the Ibex's legs. A black satin wedge-vulva is sewn between her legs and is visible on her front.*)

To conflate actual time, to make the past be actually the present by making its motions. I don't want to do that. I want the present to occur, yet that isn't anything.

The romantics thought imagination to be expression of one, that was 'discovered' — even a violation of nature.

The volatile inner rim is itself in occurrence. So has abandoned the 'real' occurrence for it.

———

A ringed horn has been broken off on the little ibex's head. But there's one left on it. Do they wait on tables?

Lying on the side, with the legs drawn up — (so) no wrestling — observation of the moon and the sun — occurs.

Is noticed that it occurred in one by some other — it's there — and there is no opposing from outside in one.

Resting, which the mind getting ready out ahead can't — as 'can rest' is separate. It is separate only — doesn't occur. Because then it's not resting.

Some other attacking one unknown there as being horrible, doing so is at the moment of that negatively regarded one not wrestling as that being observation of the moon and sun — one's dawn(?) — as being only one's observation. And so being there. 'Only' — as observation into dusk. Not after.

The element of emotion in dusk — indigo — is — ?

(A man reemerges as brown indigo butterfly)

'Suffering emergence' — in people, as a movement — seen, but not in that moment in the one, so separated in the moon and the sun's crushing to the rim as observation — where it isn't — : removes one from wrestling, the very characteristic regarded as 'horrible' (I guess) unnameably outside of society — and which the one didn't have anyway at that moment.

(Dancer rolls falling on the left side on a table.)

'Suffering emergence' seen in the people burning tar on the road at dawn, occurred in one outside only in being hated.

Running across the dew, is "Life is nothing."

There is no reason to live. Life is nothing. As they are burning the tar on gorges — laboring for the roads — as dawn's there.
Dawn being, that life is nothing. *As such.*

'One' rallies having returned as one's place, one's culture, where it has to be some *thing*.
The reentry machine, one's own rib cage even, isn't working: 'suffering emergence' is in people physically.

Thorax in collection of people 'here,' gentle flaps in isolation that's really others, not visible here, behaving in their (not one's culture's) harmony. The brown indigo butterfly flaps in isolation, from people
invisible narrative — as it moves at its center — not garden.

Thinking the mind can do anything. I thought the flesh to be fragile but didn't consider the mind to be so, it was really one's mind. As it.

Dancer: The way you say something is it.

What is spoken is utterly separate from that which is expressed.

Dancer: They are collapsing on themselves as the three parts of the dream which was known in advance by one in it.

Dancer: Yet everything is in sections. In parts, horizontal as not having relation to each other.
  They just start.

The mind: not as the characteristic of fragile or the characteristic of being out in experience only — but being experience only.

which is one's motions.

The violence one has to incorporate is too great — here — so one separates from the moon in the same sky, though the violence is not there in it.

Yet I can't; — can one — separate — as evening being in observation. That's what it would be like being 'here.' Is it necessary at all? To be in this reality, at all, even when one is being here?

As themselves making the sense of emotional as swans not moving on opal sky in flapping within it.

Emotional because flapping — a conservative is one so timid that they suppress difference
  but that person interprets conservative as representation of that which is general — which is: as allowing difference.

Anger arising from them as they are floppers, gutted — that the observation of the swans is emotion. Anger and the sight of swans aren't seen to be *their* emotion
  and their emotion is not existing in the desert where the people are starving.

Attaches a large disk of a moon on the table as if floating on the surface of the table.

Seeing the Ibex, various ones, in the brothels — is that, entirely dual in motion of it 'kneeling.' In it is a kite flying with no string on the street.
  Other ibexes (she's not singular, while being so) in the heat of day flying there; — people bathing — in city of canals; they are all over the street at dusk with other people. Shopping.

The Ibex is carried on her tray or litter by the others.

When, in mountains, in one moment they ran photographing in the faces of the people bowing, this entire stream is that.

Ibex in brothel sold, they keep a yoke on her. At night.

Coming to another unknown one in crowd.
Being imitated is this. Ibex is in brothel. Someone else, in crowd, insulting and then going to fawn on some other 'centered' one.

Compassion were it to occur in the outside — is called sympathy — in order

it not having ever been — as being brown indigo butterfly there — which occurs.
One caused to try to unite (with oneself) inside
uniting to an inner as enervated being — and it then itself isn't there — *as* enervated.

Outside invisible narrative. Outside:

Is not what is outside. The Sony even (? as it isn't theirs), the brothels, all the businesses owned by an internal minority.

(The parts don't refer back. They just start.)

(The history of order)

In the part on death — because she's young and only in life, panic wanting to get there, the crowd flocking a sense of panic in them which is *per se* their motion (singular) wanting to get there — horns begin — outside of apprehension. 'there.'
Nonexistence is 'inner': as the motion 'public.'
Enervated loss as dual: — (1) experience in one; and (2) fashion *per se*, that fashion is.
Yoked at night. — 'at night' is in one.
Wearing one's sweater on the hot night, awkward wanting to cover — the man in that early period of years saying, What will people think? — another answering, Who cares what people think, there, as there being the issue itself — being — .

Occurred then as in itself at present. The hot night being here

It is that the world burst in the extremely shallow 'here,' not even in *their* (who were the ones suffering) foreigners?
Boats speeding on the canals — at night — by McDonalds (company), fumes of white clouds of industries in dark that are only for others here, the 'foreigners' owning them.

(taking disk of moon)　　　*(warm night's disks)*

———————

I'm Trying to Describe Something:

The having to be — in oneself the strange societal schizophrenia as one's light flesh, that can hear what other people are thinking without their speaking — that is one as adolescence (: blossoming — so one has to do it, just as one has to shrivel inside in flesh later,
being that — coming together, *rather than* extreme split — in the outside configuration of the split) in one: is first cognizance *per se.*

That's also ibex. yoked. at night. separate. (as if it were not imposed by society. Here, a shape — imposed by one.)

flying outward (on the street) with the needle teeth sunk into 'others' (there being people — their being the *only* people, she's not) in outrage which is not actually arising or having any source

the 'extreme,' as others would say, conflict as being (and) that moment isn't even felt as it is subsumed in the light flesh
isn't 'ever' felt — in the sense of analyzed — then — since if it were, it wouldn't be that configuration.

One projected physically outside of oneself hearing what others were thinking without their speaking — without losing one's flesh.　　*flesh's disk*

It's back in 'inner,' the configuration as 'inner's' or separation's nonexistence in society, without that occurring — yet *as* its occurrence — and in extreme conflict which isn't felt, in arising — 'ever' as there's only 'present' in flesh.

We were playing baseball; and crouching by the mound one did see into and heard what the others were thinking.

That there isn't 'arising' except present — *is* actually felt, in the frame, the flesh — yet because it is not in cognizance at that age, it isn't 'felt' (isn't in their present) — and is being the 'extreme conflict' itself yet in being only one isolated.

Evoking 'extreme split' as one — in early stage that's formative adolescence — is seeing society (by there being no comparison in that sight). There are no comparisons.

It's a reciprocal motion — that isn't emotional (?).

That one sees oneself as extreme registration in utter peace — *is* peace. later? — but 'later' as only then (early).

The museum in the desert country displayed experience by showing strips of bark used during menstruation by women in the inferno.

One has to go to the muscles — (directly).

The muscles rigidifying, injured by the inflamed nerve so as to be not as live flesh in a person, it's not mind. It is that the mind is not told directly as it being the muscles, which the mind is. You have to go from the muscles which are without mind to the mind after. Later. is mind's apprehension?

The muscles couldn't function (which had been excruciating) at their present.

If it's ever in the mind, or not ever, it doesn't really matter? — as that *being* the mind?

Present-time not in existence, and distilled not in any pain, ever.

There isn't any registration.

I'm interested in the canals, shanties, slavery of people as in the physical phenomena — as being it.

And there isn't any registration.

To allow pleasurable experience to occur at present is a goal I hadn't considered as being experience itself (that is unknown, though pleasure has been felt continually).

The huge numbers of events haven't that cast. The cast of the man who is important, especially, precisely not that.

That isn't even occurring in the way that it seems to be.
Deer suffer.

Laboring on the road — burning the tar at dawn — lightning and
moon, of the guest workers.
Migratory — dawn?

———————

Setting is field of white larvae which extends into the viewers. Background is indigo.
The Ibex has learned by experience. Which doesn't exist in it.

(*Older and not able in flesh to go through the motions of the same
emotional syndromes any more, and so not wanting to*) — (*the savage
dogs under a moon lunging where extreme youth of ibex is flying with
legs knelt under it, one sees the little red tongue stick out*).

It's a kite but at night. The dogs attacking it ruffle its floating. The oc-
currence of the purple clouds in the night is not a syndrome even if other
clouds appear.
Eyes of the ibex are always wide open; with no eyelids. Or with eyelids
swimming across it as if the moon imitated as vision in its own sky.
— it is intellect only as occurrence. Their dichotomy is. Flecking the
leg on the table in being 'only' physical is one running toward them into
the middle so as to smash the dichotomy of the one being the same.

There was a wide plaza monumental buildings as in the capital —
sense of spaces is to empty out myself to return to myself. I herd two
identical gray horses attached at the sides by a black pole across the
space. A few people are there.
Then (a garden) someone holds up the plants on stems to show that
the stalks, floating upright on the earth's surface, were not growing on it,
were existing — with no roots (as if 'removed' 'taken' from below), indi-
cating the wildcat (yellow-spotted and had dark dipped fox's tail) present
has done this.
So I move to cut the wildcat off from leaving. It being very strong indi-
cates springing on me; a pre-dream, virtual reality vision occurs of it leap-
ing and tearing me up without this action being done in fact; so that I
move aside then not barring its path.

Having a similar dream yet recurring beginning at age fourteen. Once in it, a dog hunting me through vacant lots and tenements, nearing to attack, turned into myself — the mind going after the isolated self.

I recognized waking that this was to care for it. The isolated self had been attacking itself. Without the pair of its mind.

The people seen starving lying in rotting fruit — in the port — had had no attachment to ground either.

The wildcat (yellow-spotted . . . with a dark dipped fox's tail) now — having — taken out the basis of the plant stems.

To hear what people are thinking then.

Of the purple clouds at blackness that are as only the girl's lunging stabbing as a stick on the darkness at the dogs savagely attacking it flying.

Attacking it flying — which does not come from the girl.

Sinking its needle teeth into a dog —

They think they see blue dye not on their eyes.
In them. Inward life.
Is happy. Not enervated.

— the Ibex utters a high-pitched squealing or screaming as of a bat enraged on blackness. No eyelids.

Man appears robed
Men *like* bats their robes blowing in the darkness on trucks in the desert.

This is the hard way.
Dancer lies on table in inflated hose of cloth tunnel like white larva

Man ridiculing me, only because I am there, as a means of his having rank — to himself and another, creating that, in (as) his culture — peering at him

he looked dead *in fact*, suffering from a malaise while being dead but here.

someone coos on the sagging hulk — as if watering in light evening, did not exist conversation could wake him.

— it does not bare on green river and shining slate black river

They accepted, and when one objected, even championed his ridiculing behavior to one as that which has repute rather than their doing the real.

What is to be feared in his contemplating actions (objected to) he's therefore in in a present? Him brought to that surface of himself isn't contingent on being ridiculing. They adhere to a malaise as being order.

They would object to this view on the basis of its being real, as specific.

Jeering at those coming to death bowing while still living.
Outsiders of the crowd jeer. Members of the crowd flock to bow there.

(*This isn't a procedure of melodies. No sound even. Or compression. It rests.*)

As series which does not qualify itself, while simply continuing. *In life.* Action of theirs.

The delicate small women are in brothels for foreigners, businessmen should go to bed with horses.

There could be a circumstance in which the actions were continual and 'visible' by the people speaking of an action while doing it. People were describing an action as it was occurring and being seen: all being its occurrence. Being seen, seeing and speaking are all actions that are equal and in time. A man said, "I found the action/the movements distracting — so that I couldn't listen — I just wanted to listen to the language." I want the viewer to exist, in this distraction. Not to listen as such. So as not to re-form the action of listening, itself. At all. That one could apprehend outside of formation only.

Events have 'invented' a measure *as* space.
That occurred by their passages loosely extended not occurring any other way as life. Except that it is there.

They regard their fear as of that which is general. Suppressing — the supposed representation of difference does not actually occur.

Now that there will only be reality coming rather than from us, newspapers make impositions actually. Underwritten.

The small shops opening here selling the same pizza across the street from each other. There are no streets or night.

A band of children coming up began swarming so that the merchants nearby save them by beating the children with clubs — as children with no parents, abandoned, living on the street by the millions thieves, drug dealers, murderers are executed by the secret squads.

————

(*This is like Swan Lake but the deluded are there as themselves. As the swans* (*the transformed deluded*) *would be in their shape, they're in* theirs. *Though there's a single butterfly.*)

won't prevent child slavery. as it is necessary to the economy — say the businessmen. In night.

As it's caught and harnessed. Imprecations, not Lethe.
which could wash over one, in life.
The green bands on her face — a man at evening closing down his restaurant for good goes by men opening up a restaurant. It's light evening.

(*dryly*) That's not Lethe then, evening.

I don't see any reason why you can't do one favor after another. Do things for people continually, only. You. Underwritten.
There are chain restaurants only.

The killed activist former slave (making rugs from the age of four) isn't inversion as music having something to do with the nerve in pain in seeing inside oneself as the dye is filling one's side while flecking a leg.

Children, playmates, who don't get along, one had to give the other a gift to like her again. This doesn't seem like it's going to work.
There is a voluptuous night, one.

Underwritten. As if at day being in night
Without people there is a white road that's at night in heat — also — .

Trackers can be easily killed. Cash is exchanged. Everywhere. Borders. Panic arising from borders. Only.

(land as — it — and — 'one's' dawn)

(Butterfly as robed man with headdress covering his face)

(Robed man enters flashes, showing brown indigo markings of butterfly on the inside of his robe)

Men wearing 'veils' (face covering using headdress) also and never showing their faces — as a desert tribe, the men doing this in places as well as women. A face of a man secret to other men — is — not authority, power; as erotic to veiled women 'as' (or in being not) seen.

'there' — and — 'dawn' (one's dawn)

The veiled man meets in proximity, on the street, the unemployed whose aid has been removed in the city.

(holds ear to indicate she is hearing what he's thinking.)
A thought. Bulb rose on rim that's horizon flat sequence everywhere — opening as sequence at time — that's black rose

(A man reemerges as brown indigo butterfly in slow floating gesture)
There was the separation of 'one' from some 'outside' space (also created there), and itself seeing that 'there' *is* the separation.

The gyration (of 'one') moving away from some social place in it, was itself made-up *as* then (the instant); similarly, the 'social' place there reflected the social place.

The gyration of agitation (of the one, itself neutral even) brushed by the instrument (of one observing, itself only its same agitation in its instant) — is in order to make the socially non-normative *per se*. As a purpose. (And while being in pain at the time.)

Therefore one had to come up against the force of that regard — of impermanence — both itself and the social.

man appears robed

A man appearing yet his face is covered and he wears a headdress, only eyes — amidst canals in Bangkok — negotiated by boats, garbage, on brothels — Sony and McDonalds — is behind, having emerged from the desert.

He's the brown indigo butterfly; or within, as one existing at nights. The face covering of the man, only the eyes seen is in a present in which the women, children, are starving 'desert' 'night' outside of camps — 'chattering' in cold killing nights —

No reading. 'Chattering' at night in cold 'pass away.'

Families not traveling; they are left behind.
He begins on the hot streets elsewhere — traffic — it's not wading — canals.

————————

An antiintellectualism in being bored by this other being, in such 'other.' *per se*. One's appearing in their intellect to her lack of love. continually.

Others are loved by the one.

Viewing the problem.
In conversation, seated — beings come up struggling for being, and unloved from antiintellectualism. at all by other people — some people do.

Motor oil is a soft mirror of oil — at night a soft sea of motor oil. Brown indigo butterfly flying in it.

At his not removing the face covering and in robes and putting the part in — not being in her. Standing separate from her.

Bending in the breeze — putting the part in her; in his robes.

Ibex with the kneeling legs flying in blackness on the street — without clothes — the black soft part open.

The man who's robed has no interest, veiled — not arising from their others starving 'night' chattering.

When she's never seen his face, puts the long erection into her flying legs' opening, without cloth.

It's not that he could be veiled in front of men, is — as puritan is customary, rigor — roiling magnolia blossoms as at and as being one's breath — 'desert' 'chattering' cold is.

While he sustains heavily robed and face covering at night, also. As others in business. Or without labor. Seated on the street, by train stations.

The trunk — the veiled head on, his face covered — coming (in blackness).

Lear depended on feudal life. So tyranny can't be knowledge at present.

At earlier age, what we call being really 'out there' is having everything to lose in relation to others. Relations to only some other individuals are solely what exists here.

Yet deciding not 'to come in' (into relation with others — as dependent), later, then is a stance (of being that one — which is fake).

the convoluted being as 'out there' — by being so — : not loving that one from antiintellectualism — and as they have no money, either (funny).

They say everything
is blowing

Dog registers on the street at night as the moon does to people. Running into the middle, as 'reading,' is only physical.

(*Disk of moon is on the floor as if it is lying on the horizon of ground.*)

————————

(*Man reenters the one place covered. Another man enters at the same time dressed as that butterfly.*)

left one expressed to only grunting pigs. In everyday life to all. To whom spring has not existed.

But there is only that existing here, spring. Ordinary people wanting only power one doesn't know oneself ever.

Everyone being is a new occurrence. Everyone being only weakness, lowly (at the same time).

A man whom I met was a corpse in then being weak not even willing to converse with others.

He caters to someone as if they have rank, which gives him rank, therefore fake and reflects himself. The pod separately duplicates one.

Spring is one not having — to be a corpse — will has been misdirected.
Then a malaise sapped them, from their being corpses first. Torture at once.

She moves like the black butterfly caught in blackness.

The Ibex moves slowly as if blind beating the sides of the back indigo wall as if caught inside at a window.

. . . thinking she's the long-distance runner. She thinks she's ahead in blackness by *choosing* to run behind them, who're successful (who've hurt her). They don't even notice. They will *never* notice. So as — in blackness — no one can be seen running.

Driven by greed of pigs as of being wild, tearing each other — came — (to this state of being sapped — before one is existing).
Wanting one as no one running.
One didn't want them to accept one. Which was reducing them to re-cipients.
There can't be resolution of suffering either in any. (Resolution of these thoughts occurring is fake, as its occurrence, as is one's conflict itself.)

They may not see what this has to do with ordinary life, everyday. Wanting to silence this, to make reading as silence, is one's fascination with it.
Not seeing it in war, or in sweeping leaves as a job one held, but seeing it only in oneself

no slight movement even as the relation to others, be based on spring only. At this moment they're removing all the slats, the boards — of wel-fare protection in the country for the poor —

(*imitating*)   We call it image. The real word is reality. "Then change it." No, no, no — push the reality out.
("Then there's only image.") — as Lear — dependent.

The robed veiled man blowing in the sheets of rain at night crouched at train station — the extreme old and the extreme young are image —

All actions haven't resolution in light. A boy is bicycling?

That no one cares for anything — . Introspection is nothing — but it has to have occurred before. (To be that.)
Put one there only.

A breath in one — magnolia blossoms are roiling boils, and as their overriding being one (they are both outside opened *and as* overriding oneself) — the magnolia blossoms are present as there one's breath.
They can't be separated — from the man holding the black bud.
Trays of the roiling magnolia cups existing at one's breath — then, existing at night
too — their existing at one's breath — then, at day.

————

Field of white larvae extends into the viewers.

The approved pet as a social action, emotion from them is only possessing some other they're describing — who's lower (even when dead).

One is, in defensively in the conversation taking on the lower one's psyche, driven further outside solely.

One's a murderer then in him — outside, but as oneself really being enervated and destroyed only. The outsider is something else in fact, as he is.

silence not in 'reading' as such, as *being* reading
reading only taking place with the eyes — not — ones — apprehension.

The worms on the red wheat fields — the fields were empty — on indigo night.

The forced collectivization occurs in those having anything and those with nothing also being liquidated or shipped to slave pits, starving children having straggled off the cattle cars looking for water.

In sound, in no way, not violated either
Emotion *is* the event of society's. Or *only their* intellect is. Not one's left leg flecking slowly.

Winged man, the robes flapping — is butterfly.
The brown and indigo butterfly that holding to her in the air comes in the black is iteration (of a past).

The leg flecking — of one — in pain, as the blue dye filled one's face when I had fallen, (the image was apprehended by their cameras outside).
As oneself seeing, inside one's flesh, not on the eyes — one's seeing dye inside.

We separate in a crowd. Since I have moved away from the experience of the leg flecking — dumped on the table and seeing ('on' the eyes?) a blue pool filling within my left side and my left half of face (dumped forward on the side of the head, in pain) — *not* on the eyes at all — . Where is the action inside?
whether existing as a memory or not — as the sight had not existed in me until occurring not on the eyes — I seem to push to living as action as apprehension, yet after. Occurring by exhaustion.
It could occur some other way, but I don't know how.
The leg flecking in a blue dense pool — only — not apprehension while occurring, or exhaustion yet.

When finally one is breathing on one's thorax — a breath into it only, just barely breathing (shallow on it) — I notice one wants people to care about one, and have to push to physical exhaustion. in fact. of anyone. That's of people noticing *anything*. Tears occur but as relief as the boundary of exhaustion. But hopeless because there is no rest in anything.

Though dumped the leg flecking seeing the blue pool — had no exhaustion, or apprehension which was later clear
But one can't go back. Disk of moon is removed.

————

Both groups producing interior tyranny only — the woman producing their description of the 'feminine' (herself) as curtailment, as self-content, so that people swoon on it (the curtailment) as her, is *their* same interior tyranny —

It was negated by being simply intolerance — without senses. Yet the insult tore one apart. (Nothing's negated.)

The leg flecking — seeing (not on the eyes) the dye in oneself — one could see some other in an action, their being, there.

There's nothing to worry about in the day yet one can't rest, having to do daily routine of life, jobs.

One's physical body cannot stand the inner nature of the world.
(as that is its inner nature because it's perceivable.)

The two, the hooting figures leaping — and the blossomed-tree(d) space, shopping, are the same. They are turned inward. In one.

carrying food — bouquets — for the live couple

(Hooting figures roping in those fleeing — yet the crowd seeing wanting to come in, bowing)

Twinned: hooting figures encircling in 'one's' entering — and here 'one's' in spring, quiet elation out only, we were shopping, for the wedding dinner; salmon, wine, cakes. For the couple.

In the warm blossomed-tree(d) air the animal heads and the figures shouting leaping with both feet in the air can be greeted as (being) an insect had come up, bucket, while swimming to one.
bowing people, to entering dying
that's in spring itself

'One's' physical body — our together slow shopping, out — being turned in — buying cakes, wine — resting.
the small movements of shopping — spring'd
and the small movements of hooting figures leaping — one

(as their being — accustomed to small movements — of these, spring'd.)
(We're used to small movements of artificial made violence in one. Twinned.)

Pets too were just in spring. Pets in society.

Now it's dinner in light.

Out of the window a bird is singing outside of exhaustion only — there can be none.

(Regardless if this occurred at some other time.) Theirs is leaping figures — out on the street, entering. — for a bird to sing outside — spring only

————

(Women are being abusive to Ibex. They put her muzzled mouth down into bowl of milk as she's kneeling resting on her arms and knees, her arms curved backward on the floor as if they are antelope legs. Ibex wears muzzle.)

In front of it who's lying on the floor by the bowl of milk.

(removes muzzle)   One horn had been broken off the Ibex's head but one curved long horn remains.

Are there legal sentences? Beginning to drift, the heavy head crashes the muzzle dipping it in the bowl of milk.
Beneath her leather muzzle are the green tattoo bands, the red small tongue

Man on back of truck blowing flapping, arising from the desert dawn — starving —
their dying from chattering at nights.

migration — too many people born — to gorges —
At present people are the main export — one existing there — a condescension from some one to one that is violence to others

The dogs jumped up in the blue night of the alley — as I was running — trying to seize me, tearing in the air at me, I had the perception then of them that they were growing older — that I was also of course — but that it was the dogs as growing older perceptible in the instant in the blue night.

Robed veiled man unseen blowing robes — on truck tray from dawn-desert — going
Merely subjective is what is then her posturing *per se*, imperialistic as the movement itself is.
(She sticks her tongue out at the Ibex. Then says spitefully referring to

Ibex as the "one" mentioned:) Not to allow one to be, either in the setting or in oneself.

The man in the back of the truck swaying is not her inside action, bringing the man to dawn from her being turned on the table with the dye in one seeing one's own inside without that being on the eyes. Seeing inside arose from effort — any?

Underwritten — is having a patron, such as Exxon or Standard Oil, which is unrelated to either of the instances, of the girl or man, and underwritten because it is these being unrelated yet there.

———

The form (not form, but procedure) of account by
monks and nuns at night as to what caused them
to decide to leave the world and seek the Way:[1]

I had a friend whom I cared about yet had only a minor relation to her my being regarded as supportive only. She hadn't noticed my characteristics. But I thought she might some time. She mentioned herself as central based on being in a group, yet saying I was in a group in a negative sense, dependent (in another group, which had not accepted her, she said) — whereas I sought to destroy groups — only. I sought to destroy groups — and my one quality? I realized life was nothing.

———

The brown indigo butterfly and the robed covered man are the same. They are him. They are present experience.

Not to allow one to be, either in the setting or in oneself.

———

The man being a war criminal and an outcast and dead and described had been viewed based on the one viewing him being in a group. As if that were all right.

Her viewing herself as central based on being in a group was accompanied by being publicly described by another as feminine — the implication being setting her apart there from other women.

Whereas the definition is a dependent category — in the setting.

So that one had to be bereft, in social implication, on several levels at the same time. One would have to have been born dependent, without this having occurred — which it hasn't — in order to be there.

One could not and cannot want it.

(*To seek to destroy groups — as they are illusion, are white larvae observing dawn — is one's only trait.*
So one cut one's hair and left the world.)

The warring sides found that children could kill easily having no conscience yet.

Little boys were recruited by the warring sides, who would kill with AK-47s, finding they liked their elders groveling begging, and then loot as their reward.

––––––––––

Veiled man — as the desert garb of their men and women, the men not showing their faces even to each other — entering brothel by canals releases the muzzled girl green-banded by carrying her out a window upstairs.

seen robes billowing

"Puritanical" and that veiling is inhibited (introverted) are dual as our notion, here? Other/as oneself — as such — is a weird denial of the senses.

Where at dawn on gorges burning the tar — migratory labor on roads — as it (one and the man being there) being at dawn only — is neither one as him or ever without him. There.

(love) This one *other* seeming to be one — yet there being no resemblance between *their* lives and nature — is not introversion.

plot and having one is serial in the outside setting. which implies a lidless eye when awake. At night, veiled young man in headdress desert nomad arriving from starving people, is not related to Exxon or Bechtel while entirely affected by them. In this case, and is written for them. The same as the magnolia blossoms are both the outside opened *and as* their overriding oneself.

So one cuts one's hair and leaves.

———————

(*A huge black rose is carried in or floats in on wires so that it is in the air floating forward.*)

(*The action collapses inward as the people speaking to each other impinge on action*)

I'd been flecking the left leg on the table and beside me later an old man vomiting, groaning, not complaining — as not even the crowd flocking to him, (close to dying).

The pinned shackled legs held kneeling, her black part there as a bud — trembles — the man enters the brothel robes having been filled with the breeze as if sails *then* when outside.
Before arriving the robes filling in the breeze are sails, rather than *him* being conveyed then.

The blue dye filling within my left side earlier — and my seeing it inside not with my eyes, somewhat on the eyelids in flickers, as they dumped me to have me falling on the table —
I had no thought or feeling — though in pain — I was clear (this not done with my mind — there was no death or life, the left leg flecking outside while the leaden blue pool filled in me as I fell), that of not being in life ever — and being here — therefore curiously happy.

Where is the base if his people are starving of one's living?
In first realizing the fact of death as a child one sees inside oneself not as memory or observation. (Not with one's mind.) Their laboring on gorges — as the reverse or the same — of dawn — is life is nothing.
Yet it was so painful that one was turned inside-out.
The interior (which is invisible real action) is interpreted — by its *being* invisible — there is no other interior than actions.
(*One's living isn't based in the sun's bulb crushing the black cradle that's the sky even.*)

———————

One says, I thought we have no other relation to anything than friend-ship.

Ibex who wears bright dark red lipstick opens her mouth in silent laughter.

Ibex is picked up at her ankles and shoulders by the dancers — held there, she is straight in the air.

The trembling of her black part — the man's robes filling as if sails outside

her part had not been entered

————

The hearer has a view of herself on other occasions but, as it happens not then. Though the ghost mirrors her already existing interior conflicts — her being outside but really only (having) to protect that one (who is someone else actually)
 yet the 'ghost' while being the interior conflict is someone, itself — not even that person who died then (thus who isn't 'in death' now) — my mind is phenomena

Hearing or 'viewing' 'only,' the viewer or listener became a medium into whom the 'ghost' of this stranger entered. The hearer had anger and vengeance then that is the one outside who had killed others, so can't be retrieved.

The dead man came to the empty hearer via the speaker who was cre-ating sentiment as a view of herself
 felt by the hearer as violence — which is not interior violence
(It is not interior violence for the speaker — regarding the speaker — at the time it's occurring)

The expression (by the speaker) — of one not 'in death' now (the ghost), (rather is so only when that one died) — was a catalyst, causal; one may say only as the already existing interior conflicts of the hearer — but really it was some other thing
 oneself as some other thing (only)

The black butterfly on black night is introverted, as his supposed infe-
rior nature is.
    so the liquid black (night) isn't a past — one
    in resting in it has no present/future. (And as seen by us.)
    (Not being a future by itself, it can only be a present/future.)

This now is not the one who'd killed, it is some other known to one
(the one who'd killed was outside one's experience, open also). Outside
the night is the blue. Baiting the person's future nature as not "gregari-
ous" — who being in the night past by it being afterward, a later — is the
action. There's only action.

The baiting describing his nature and (an other) one's (the double) as
inferior, as not "gregarious" — one is being in 'an' black night.
    So the black past only appears (as such: forward/future).

One's nature being inferior to (as one is not being in) crowds, the night
'appears' backward receded, but 'as' being the base — as *being* action of
night/forward *per se*
    one's (other) and his nature, the double loses the way to apprehend, as
such, even being bottom rim of blackness.

Why if his (him being unknown to one) and one's natures are criticized
from childhood as inferior in not being "gregarious" (as if an entity in
being valued by others) — someone's nature 'becomes' (?) an action only
there, as if 'becoming' 'an' night, that being liquid black, is blur of black
on the base of the sky?
    Someone else is suspicious.

The inner duplication of the world outside includes someone whom
one didn't know propelled by a speaker. — The 'one outside' and not
being 'in death' except when they had died — (who gets in one) is 'their'
mind as only phenomena.
    Inner duplication is occurring at the same time of a man who is alive
and is the same as oneself.
    If one is in the black liquid present that would overlap these persons.
They wouldn't occur. in one.
        but one likes them living in frenzy
        at the same time amusing

that is one

The leg kicking out in back (attached to the back, which roils) at the line of the blue and of night — then on the flying roil kicks again (at another figure flying up). The leg on the roil/being out from it.

One kicking the gills, the leg on the back of the person who kicks touches the flying front of the other person.

One's roiling form flies straight forward with one leg kicking from its back.

In one Nōh play a dead warlord who'd in life killed many people can return only once from hell to visit his small son. The figure changes his dress when he's seen to be (is revealing himself as) that (ghost). He sings, is impermanence, withdraws to return to his hell.

I wonder why seeing the ghost that is oneself (recognizing that is oneself dead, as one is [there] in the past — so the present is the same as the past/future) — oneself who is someone else, enabled someone else (an actual ghost, which is mind phenomena) who'd been sent into me to be released (by not being in me any more).

The only field that's real again is what happens.

The deer fish swam. Small deer with only one horn on face so it has no legs.

There is forest of deer fish swimming or forests even, there. Small faces and so with no legs.

For they have one horn in the center having no legs. Oneself. Curled humps now are the deer as gills. *Actions would be the same thing as a dream (without there having been one).*

deer night. deer night. at night there being no swimming as not being a pair at all

not swimming, one doesn't either. They are interiorly entirely deer, in their physical being and appearance, yet no legs in their actions there. One is also.

Pressed, into being deer, yet there is no appearance or characteristic of such. As them one doesn't observe being a deer then.

That's why I thought she was a friend.

But it also does not matter if she isn't?
These are the same. But pairs don't say it.

The pairs never say it, though they can.
A part of the pair says it but then only to that one.
Deer fish sail without a fin in mass.

Night hasn't forests (itself).
Rumpled finless deer sailing (— with one joint once). Two say it.

I'm going to give up observation of people.

————

one other's kicked by the leg; then another is kicked by the other leg on
a roiling furls — (the leg) coming up to that one (from the back on its roil).
The curled square (sitting) young monk in black robes with the yellow
strands of snot having emerged from his nose there in the outside blue air
— the yellow filaments are still attached in the black lung (cage that bil-
lows softly — in spring)
early morning yellow filaments attach in the blue.

As those not showing signs of starvation, millions starved, their grain
exported, were beaten by their officials (for hoarding — apparently, as
they were not visibly starved) —
Writing individual single poems in a series of sentences of prose — is
'transgressing' poetry and prose as being 'bled onto' each other. Visual
only. Always it is conflict in 'one.'
Bringing the other culture to be inner (which is not one's) is the pres-
ent.
(Present time as being action.)
Why is 'that we have to die' (considered for the first time, when young)
the 'other' culture? — in which one was, but can't be of it
so adopting 'it' 'visually' — so an outer blossom (a single one on a
tree) is one (animate but not mind)
a blossom is animate — only.

What is the relation to the dream occurring only at the moment in being
in the waking state — as suppressed it couldn't exist except as impinging

(at the present) so had no whole (in occurrence as dream —) ? — to being driven

the arm having been suppressed as flesh the physical being has existence — its suppression — which may be spring, as time — to out there?

The magnolia cups (blossoms and buds roiling) — so that one's breathing occurs — at their roiling — the day has no separation or night in it.

By the night being so bright — yet at the same time as day —

want to get to the double place which is *as being* separate *per se*.

To soothe the flesh around the nerve but which may have the effect of suppressing dreams, and the dreams beginning to impinge, they break in on ordinary waking state, occur at the same time, not remembered

If the impinging shred from dream couldn't occur in sleep, when was it occurring — yet the shreds seemed to be of a whole, from some whole — in waking life at the moment of its impinging? So it never has time to occur except at present moment.

The shreds appearing to come from one — the double is entirely separate and isolated by being impinged

as (at that time — so: in time) magnolia blossoms roiling on budded trees — impinge on one's ordinary breathing/ location, separately. Not on one's seeing.

Seated on a bench in heat in the capital, there slender young men almost naked playing ball in front of one

slender without shirts playing ball, their hair cut short as if in punk fashion that's with Vs on their heads, they look the same

marines playing ball in heat in the capital — in another left arm

One's left arm dies only some times. Then revives.

One having been pinched by the nerve — as the black butterfly

A woman seen (and therefore seeing herself *from them*) as the separation between men and women, maintaining their division and therefore having status above other women — her seen as dependent there, which is valued *per se*

'relying on emotion,' as being the conception of what people are —

later is only "opposed" (rigidity as a social mind form) to the hump com-
ing in the black night, as analytical function *per se*
    that it is *there*, the hump, is analytical itself

    It isn't people.
    One's interior as imitating intimately as 'their' (others') culture is the
indigo brown butterfly finally. As *this*. As if it is the present
    as if that transgresses one's nature, as neither being — the isolated
night below and above
    at the same time overriding
    by they're both being in the isolated night only — and below and
above

    Though the moon is reduced and isolated, is as if bled on the line
(only, which is being double)
    so: as their playing ball in the capital in light glare of day — at same
time as the reduced line

    The slender marine who is his motions — one, as a job — one's left
arm is useless in night. In heat and light glare 'at' day. They're running on
the field playing ball in the capital
    it matters so these are not double. Nor reduced. Not isolated either.

    Crescent moon that's the bottom rim of the moon's luminous eclipsed
globe, faint except for its rim — its illumined rim rolls in the blackness, as
if a boat
    at night people walk, when one is walking toward them — the moon's
crescent rim floating itself an illumining boat.

    Slender marines playing ball in the capital in dim heat as day — for the
first time?
    bursts past blackness — both — playing
    no violation of nature occurs in one blackness
    a pair that's blackness, in it
    blackness is being alive only. Why?

    and so it is early (as time) — is free of one's where one placed it
    blossom blackness isn't free of one's mind — so one returns to oneself.
having been torn.

Not to suffer — at all — is *not* friendship existing? One isn't suffering, at all.

A man having an ego stream sent out to them has authority. They are responding to his having a position, apparently unable to distinguish this from his quality of apprehension

But if there were no nuts in the robes, people would not fawn. No nuts and no robes, no fawning. or no nuts and robes, no

The nuts in robes has a viscous density moving slowly — in blossoms; so: in time — the spinal fluid taking a long time to move in anyone — one has to hang one's head, the ball in black — where the fluid moves. in the black.
One is an elephant — elephants in a stream shooting water then. When the spinal fluid has moved.

The will that something not be action as viscous density of the nuts in robes
the characteristic of (ones) order is violent. but without seeing the nature of their actions, any.
Viscous density, slow insular opinion, as of the nuts in robes eliciting catering and being beside a black moon.

Dream of meeting someone and, before but at the same time of the occurrence, having the thought that "all of life is void" which I knew she'd want to hear rushing up to her, she was smiling, nothing said.
There were three parts to the dream, the future in the dream known so that it was occurring at the same time first. Spitting in a donkey's eye was in the third part so it was as if it *has* occurred — early in the dream before it *has*. There's an incredible freedom, not having to worry.
An action that the other woman would find difficult. (She is good at other things.)
Yet not action *there*, by being there.

Frogs plateaus moon on black — there
Outside the dream — only — . That's what this is. No, in *it* too. (Which wasn't in it.)

I think the essence of Nōh drama is the ghost (one's own dead self)

passing before the live one (one viewing); and so aware there is no distinction of present, being alive as the same as being dead (the past/future?).

This occurs by one's dying having been before one realizes being alive there.

This isn't different from some other, not alive, being in one — existing in time neither past, present, or future — as one's mind's phenomena?

The lung — by itself.

A black lung as ones wing is at the blue line of dark. There's a blue line at night.

He hasn't been privy to very many of my laughing fits.

"I'm ready for more," he says melodiously. jetting translated by an ocean in day.

As a child, I used to have the lung by itself in black — I'm beginning again.

The nuts in robes sandbags carried by hand (by others) one is shooting at the moon black racing in day a sail.

Even with dignity they carry the nuts in robes, sandbags handled for him.

On the shore people carrying baskets of coal weighed on yokes of sticks on their shoulders crawl in lines on black mounds, the coal air dense to be not visible even is. The stacks of factories pour out black into the tenements.

No isolated experience could exist — to 'see' that experience. It can't even occur.

Zoned-out like grandma like groundhog? What did she say?

Mt. ears are wet. The wet ears hear.

Whereas the night (past) (being only present) had been an action of the future only, the slender marine playing ball in the hot blossoming glaze of the capital — the other space is of no night occurring in moonless 'brown.'

Because it's 'brown' — 'no' 'night' *occurs*.

The slender marine is the Other's trainer only action being a past.

The lines crawling carrying coal on mounds in the poisonous fumed sky stacks pouring is no past and not a present — *was* then — at all

The sandbags that are his nuts hauled by the dignified catering people are at the same time as the sky stacks pouring — in (past) brown that's now.

Early on, small children working twelve hours a day in a factory, as they can climb between the machines, some ground in them
they aren't carrying the sandbag-nuts in blue — we all have to be operated on or die

so little realized — occurs — as 'no' 'brown' 'night' — then — the sandbags handed within the robes up a mountain — 'at' night is, (separate).
one's lung is still too there. one isn't realizing either there very much.

————————

contemplative life that is world instigated by

— plagued by borders — girls, being young having nights which is huge (the small experience that is night fitted into theirs) — and alone 'woman seated at tea' with vast brilliant shining dress not even light playing in it which is rich/itself a middle(?) as if thighs shone through it within and being the landscape — that isn't the future of the girls
they have sensation of never having worried

————————

The huge luminous dress outside — it is not one, yet seated at tea — pearl billows seated outside — resting;
— there is no social especially there either.
not an extension of the pearl luminous dress outside seated at tea —
competing is separate, a form of *joie de vivre* — running by anyone —
he flags her through
as if a race were being at tea — as that being utterly separate

————————

The veiled man putting his part in the black bud — but which had not been entered, this had not occurred — which trembles — his robes filling in the breeze are sails before coming there.

There are no habits — are not related to his entering

The crawling lines on the black mounds of the moon
a lung ones wing lighting on coal humps, no pair there

———————

The black bud now as thorax:
The rib cage out of alignment, askew, the black bud can't breathe —
yet it is thoughts occurring earlier — therefore not causing, not causal,
myself to forget how to breathe

Not causal thoughts — the leaden arm heavy with pain was the present

So one cannot unravel the habits that form thoughts
One imagines one cannot — that is the earlier thought at present. To
forget anything is the leaden arm in pain at present. Waking unable to
breathe that are not from a thought itself — is not from habit either —

If there is no time, there's no forgetting. The rigid being in present — as
corrosive habit. I have to — not forget — or adhere — to the present even
One can't remember physical pain, after it's over. At some point
after, my mind was (this no longer occurs) awake destroying my body
— my leaden arm in heavy pain (again) is not earlier thoughts endlessly
in any present, this one — and it is contingent on this occurrence/these
past occurrences? The *arm* remembers.
One with the leaden arm is in this occurrence — wakes at night forget-
ting how to breathe so that one turns on the stomach, making it breathe
— holding the left arm off the bed, one does not come from earlier
thoughts at present, the leaden arm isn't unraveled as a condition.
So it can't be unraveled — is the brown indigo butterfly — ever
It appears not to be unraveled.
Memorize. No logic. The butterfly being there is one easily.

I realized what it is to me and that it's all right to put my secret con-
cerns into it and work on it seriously (though it isn't of value). It occurs to
me that plays now may be the really *meant* terrain that is 'away from,'
not accessible to, the outside invasion, which seems to be encroaching on
me. No one cares about plays now. Because no one cares about actions.
So it being public is the most inner act.

The thief and the flute player are invisible — very specific.
Thoughts are introduced for the first time.

The huge black rose is plucked down.

————

I dreamt, when I was in fact traveling, that I met Carla — but having nothing to do with "traveling," happening to — and the sole thought, nothing said, as a revelation and alleviating, "there's no reason (that people can) not to enjoy people/that it's possible/enjoyment of people."
The dream about Carla is information.
Not 'As material *for* something therefore' — as it's not *for* words, this.
While traveling, I saw Bill Viola's video, *The Meeting*, where three women meeting and greeting, no words (the 'scene' taken from a 'prior scene,' of a painting, so they're dressed in sense as subliminal of earlier clothes) — are an original occurrence of two seconds which is stretched and takes place in twelve minutes 'giving it?' the greeting a sense of being heavenly and intense, uncovering what occurs in actions. At all. Ever. It's 'charged' as being seen merely. —

Only earlier thoughts in any present, this one.

To unravel requires unrooting thoughts which I didn't have then — have only at present yet not as thoughts now but only as muscle responses from them. So where does thought occur, in the future?

(*The arm hanging off the bed — meeting in it the thought occurring that people can/it is possible for them to/enjoy people — the dream was separate.*

Meeting and the dream — in it — are separate)

————

A view of Nāgārjuna. Being merry is experienced as no authority.
Authority is an imposition — contrary to people's experience, of their occurrence. And (their) they're perceiving occurrence.
Authority *per se* negates there being the nature of one — in anyone. In observation of action, observing is not in an activity.

Beginning is not separate from occurring and in that nothing's being in cooperation even.

If it is a condition in it — gaiety emerging — is impermanence

Can people herding others in garbage forgive them? No.

They can't be herding. Can one imitating be oneself?

(*As the bodies are being swept in surf and wind forward:*)

Whatever comes from my mind is just fine, *he says.* (Change your mind.)

Can one herd them? — they can't be herding themselves — by themselves — by oneself.

One herding all by oneself. Suffering emergence — is an imposition

To say that anyone cannot govern themselves is to seal the entrance — of crowd flocking to bow — theirs

Dreamed awake the entrance was sealed — for them

There's only jeering.

Oneself is only dreaming — in seeing. There is no entrance anywhere for one

There are no actions that unseal the entrance

We're getting to the point where experience is incomprehensible.

Any experience is incomprehensible — Even that which one is in

Friends come.

(*motions for them to get away*)   There have to be no guide — for children. At all. The actions of mother — who has no love — are contrary to anything, to all, have no indication for child — who is out there, before words.

Come to meet without indication.

The child comes passing through the battlefield in which there is no indication except the reflection of those same actions. Suggestion of initiated action.

Those being met are neither child nor any of the others — or oneself.

There's no such thing as there being ability in anyone, that doesn't exist.

Seeking to destroy groups is not based on one?

This stream is something infusing itself with substance and that's the only substance it has. As it being in perception *per se*.

Yet — then, not from one's apprehension — the night being at dawn is the same. As in compelled actions.

The people migratory, working on the roads, crawling out from under the corrugated zinc pieces under which they live — where they are on the gorges at dawn burning the tar: *dawn* is — life is nothing.

That dawn is that. (At present.)

That one could supposedly subvert imperialism only as commentary — yet this is ineffective — rather than one being that which is reversed/which is being subverted *by* imperialism. And exists apprehending itself.

The latter is action that is its motion (doesn't exist — 'there' at any place as a sole entity in the series or sequence or whole — nor in any other form than its moves) by not asserting its content simultaneously or sequentially. Authority *is* ignorance.

Her black bud — crouching open — the pink tulip buds (on trees) roiling in the air — one opens there.

———

(*Robed man face covered, stands for a moment with robe blowing up around him like Marilyn Monroe standing over the grate with her dress blowing up.*)

A child imitates in space certain motions and shapes derived from earlier incomprehensible relations conveyed by others. Motions are created beside (as if 'by') themselves, such as the motions of running. One's imitation of minute physical gestures (yet) as language is utterly separate from someone's or one's conceptionalization, which is equally empty. The motions have no generalization (have no language, which is what they are here). Conceptualization (interpreting what?) is in a void as observation. Occurrence does not bring these even with each other; in occurrence (of either at the same time) they ('motions' and 'conceptualization') are utterly separate, are gone there, and one realizes that.

There is no reciprocal gesture

held apart, so that all experience — which is memory even — at present
is not observed — there is no observation 'there' — (motions one makes
registering as memory are not observed — in the sense that observation is
something else, occurring entirely by itself)

Cognition (which seems first, after) and events may occur at the same
time but separately — in experience.

Obliterating observation by it being sole and experience by it being
sole.

The black bud beating and being his butterfly — giving up his mind

This occurs easily by simply giving up one's mind — and the outside —
not hanging on. (Yet one has to hang on to write it?)

if the visual is bled on — to one — it's the other one of the pair — the
crawling lines carrying on the black mounds with moon is — ?

lightning humps — coal.is — outside. at all.
the 'scrawl' (writing) being their outside — in the world.

In fact alone 'woman seated at tea' outside — one — can't be that
there — but is.

Baiting the person's future nature as not "gregarious" —   is the ac-
tion. 3 A.M. itself is. —   blossoms
(my) on —   from cliff — flying — with tiny children — where horns
begin — *before* apprehension — when that isn't one's experience *as* a child
    and so seated at tea outside

The green-banded incarcerated — freed — is in the night by the bats
who are so many the green-bands swims in a sea of them.

The green-banded does not seek to destroy groups. I seek to destroy
groups — that is only present-time activity.

Now the green-banded can hear what people think yet she hasn't suf-
fered.

Her black bud motoring.

There is no "inner" here that is different from their actions.

whether they are sights and experiences in the dream that have no
words, are before words, or given as/in words *after* it
In those flocking to bow with the glib jeering photographing them —
the flocking have no rim or place as that only.
They don't see it on their eyes? Their dancers leap there once.

Giving up the outside as 'conversation' and at the same time giving up
the interior 'conversation' occurs *in* the 'viewing' of performing (these
becoming the same).

(death as social —   shown to oneself —   light whirling, some try to
run away, are drawn back in) there is no social —   yet one's articulated

---

the osprey — would curve (to fly up — but can't / when going straight
up — stall / then drop like a stone — letting out a cry
then would curve / fly straight up — stall in the aeronautical / then
straight-falling drop
crying

woman at tea outside — pearl luminous billowed dress — seated
outside
in woman seated outside — then — at tea — one
Outside only there drinking tea. Blossoming trees everywhere in light,
sheets of rain come down beside the blossoms on trees; are at their sides,
which is in its midst.

One's breathing in one's lowest frame is in the structure throughout of
trees everywhere blossoming and slabs of rain outside beside these.

Not dependent on feudal life
even (myself) blind as seeing inside not on the eye dye which is visible
to the outside viewer
half-moon *in fact* as it isn't half-moon / dawn

Something about the having to die later but specifically having to live
until then only (apprehended when young) initiated then being beside

streaming cars to throw oneself in, at dusk with fallen leaves — in gutters
and streets of fall leaves, the adults behind the wheels are wary
    bumper-to-bumper traffic — roaming — at kid

There's a connection of this to there being no rules, the assuaging of
this by there being no rules.

Wanting to stow away, desperate (as condition of then, young) to stow
away — on ships — checking the newspapers for the arrivals and depar-
tures.

    kid then walking beside streaming cars in dusk — at the present only
    motion in space of events — dawn is dusk
    Outside(-events)is bounced to be occurrence. itself.

    (here) to seek to please and to receive attention as the only thing there
is — so if one is not receiving attention one is nothing

There is no relation between events and events. (Their) occurrence at
present is that relation.

    Notion that conceptualization and action are separate — one is not one
    as bounding out of one — not as viewing *life* as inferior

    to realign *their* narrative in the sense of the writing being that separa-
tion — one is not one —
    as bounding out of one

Girls who menstruated used bark. Wear your sweater. Breathing
against the bats, a million seeking food. Work on the roads.

On cliff ledge below plateau of multitudes of tiny children seated — tiny
children on one's feet fly on (out from) cliff ledge

On gorges/at dawn burning tar there only night being one's actions
movements — yet 'at' *their* dawn yet not a 'past.'

One steps aside, not barring the wildcat one. In the dream, the wildcat
had removed the roots. the 'basis'

Iron lung, that must be it — we always heard about them. Need dimes.
They flew at night, breathing deeply — the little flimsy lungs inflated.
And by them, as if in the middle of an ocean, the heavily veiled robed
man abandoned halcyon put his part in the black bud of green-banded.

*One is in the crowd flocking to bow in leaping shouting dancers as flow-
ing robed-men's brown and black butterflies flapping on field.*

Saying they are people in garbage who choose to be
they dead fighting as guerillas, their *children* are guerillas — to seek to
destroy groups is a limit. Why is 'that we have to die' considered for the
first time — one blossom only — mocked outside *per se?*
— yet as if seeing on one's retina what is inside (being the limbs) is nei-
ther one — or the limbs
to seek to destroy groups (one's)

*Because all belonging — in the contemporary society — is the creation
of actions that are the society — any is to violate actions*
*Violating one's own actions in oneself — inner — dawn — as volatile
rim, only, then.*

Present as disjunct *per se* only — *that* space / time cannot be 'their'
narrative — or one's. *Event is between.*

**Woman is sarcastic responding to other woman and at the same time she
is being derisive to Ibex:**

I must be a Sunday painter.
The iron lungs and the lead-pipe-for-an-arm are pride-riding where
there isn't even that. There is no night at that pride-riding except taking
in the firmament.

The robed man billowing as a worm. Brushes against bats, breathing.
The green-banded, now separated by crowds, freed not from him (it
not needing to be from him, whom she loves — yet lost in the streaming
crowds they are separated from each other) — working on gorges, seeks
the Way. (*To Ibex:*) (You're just trying to get revenge. Stand and fight.)

*Dancer (speaking to the Ibex:) You're just trying to get revenge. Stand
and fight.*

Notes

Deer Night was instigated by the idea of a complete transformation of *The Tempest*, a construct of Western and Asian conceptions as the motions of the mind, only the mind *being* action or phenomena *as* writing. The intention was for the work to be a state of freedom (eventually), subverting capitalism's 'imperialism' from the inside.

See "Silence and Sound/Text" and "Footnoting."

1. Margaret Helen Childs, *Rethinking Sorrow, Revelatory Tales of Late Medieval Japan* (Ann Arbor: Ann Arbor Center for Japanese Studies, University of Michigan Press, 1991).

:: *Friendship*

for Lyn Hejinian

the doesn't overwhelm. the night.

———————

—as the white blossoming tree: as it isn't occurring
'isolated' 'one'

arriving white 'blossoming' tree as one 'only'

———————

outside of one 'isolated'—in the ocean, work that is not 'its' capacity.

moves 'at' night—isn't 'their' action

———————

that of no ground (on which one walks)—with huge ravens, cawing—
from one's side—in blossoming trees only.

everywhere. huge ravens—cawing flying—only in blossoming trays
blown—one.

———————

—from one's side—in blossoming trees only
everywhere only

black. in blossoming trees. not in black sky—one walks.

———————

ego streaming from him (almost visible) eliciting people catering to him
is not like black from one's side flying in blossoms

———————

'murderous' day—not like sea in black—being filled
with calm in which the filaments
sail—in both. (the sea in black and day.)

——————

sail in vegetation—in one—(and: 'a' sail)

blossoming trees everywhere. 'they' couldn't (as 'that not being able
to') make distinctions

——————

aren't paired and no sky in blossoming
pair as blossoming and 'one'—only

the ocean 'having' hawks on it beating

huge black ravens flying—in blossoms only—from one's side—and
black ducks which aren't flying have wild eyes on water [at the same time]

——————

the land is paired as single—as people
—fish and birds in one's hell

—paper mills—steel factories
destroying—only—rubble— 1.2 billion living

—only—coal thorax night's
brown in the hell—land

——————

is one's thorax-banded—pump—as it's in the black sea spring—in it?
is spring in the thorax—one's—people crushing the land out of
need?—not one's in *it*.

spring in black sea—of the held thorax?

———————

the land and 1.2 billion living are in
a—one's—thorax—chemical wasteland in

paper mills, steel factories, coal the
waste acid pours as sky into the huge

river—and sky pairs in visible hell of
no seeing and living—workers

in rubble—cubicles—coal thorax floated on barge
wakes

———————

hell land brown night's thorax
rubble—living only

there's only living (?)—work is
night—too—wasted mills'—one's—'not'

—as too—

_____

brown ill—coal—cubicles—'not' one is also
weight
tugs—wake—coal sloughs—only

aren't paired and no sky

_____

one's—'brown.' no night.

gray tenements
—stacks
yet

_____

Surrounded by horizontal vast plains of cities, mountains, coal mines, on
river—I dreamt about a man I hadn't seen for ten years—we were going
to go to lunch. I was trying to drive him—to unite him—with my grand-
mother, who is dead and who in dreams always turns her face, facing to
the side unspeaking. In the dreams I always know that she is dead.

In this one, I didn't know she was dead, and her face was turned for-
ward to me. The man's face was turned to the side from me, and then he
didn't go to lunch.

Waking, I feared he'd died. (When I returned home he phoned and
said "I had a dream about you. I dreamed we were going to go to lunch.
But then we didn't . . ."

I realized the dream was my mind investigating spatially. It was not
that the man was dead. It was that my grandmother *wasn't*, spatially.
They're on the same horizontal space/time.)

———

gorges—horizontal lightning people

———

night rain on 'brown'—[stacks waving—there's 'no' night]—one is
in
horizontal lightning people

———

horizontal lightning—making night

'no' 'night' occurs—then. one.

[where there was] 'no' 'night' as there are people. at all there, stacks
waving
that's on people however then

(at all there—is horizontal 'there')

———

humps rainless moon—

[not at the same time] no stacks waving—there's 'night'

on humps moon flowing horizontal
high

———

separation of dark humps and
wild moon—when

(with) no horizontal lightning in the
space

neck in it—one's and the high night
is in the humps

———————

people in lines on cliff carrying coal—lines on black humps
black humps of horizontal lightning [not at the same time]

coal—one—'no' relation of work as people crawling lines on cliff
and—to—black humps moon.
is black humps moon.

———————

coal humps—people lines crawling on cliff—on humps
'no' 'night' occurs—then. one.
night's horizontal lightning people [not at the same time] [space]

is

———————

people carrying in lines on cliff—people crawling carrying on brown
mounds [not at the same time]

one's—go inward—not night's
yet

————

relation of ('not') dying—to people crawling in lines carrying on
mounds seen—ones
and [not at the same time] river's black humps people as lines crawling
carrying
as river

————

not association but space changed
—black humps rainless—only

————

as prior in brown tenements falls strand river—all no
—social—space ever—thick flowing up flat

[water]

having formed argument as one's being [for one, in infancy
—reciprocating—if not(?)

—'not' as falls cubicles tenements.

brown falls—small thorax filled—spouts falls
[at the same time then]

————

decks—thick

lines crawling on a mountain to eat at night

————

birds—wakes

cubicles tenements sides pouring factory chemicals from spout—falls—.

brown small thorax fills—not being in oneself—or in them—falls
strand [and] flat water

only living having to die as being that isn't at the same time—one's
brown small thorax—is falls horizontal? there
only

what difference do mountains make?—
_____

'at' night not carrying

one's walking 'brown' night—(walking on water)—people crawling in
lines up
what's the relation to its existing [at the same time]?

_____

'can't face'—(in present is 'at the
same time') the lines of people crawling on coal

carrying—isn't 'facing' the night (?)
land spouts of mills as the same

land—'not'—on—1.2 billion—'facing'
space

one doesn't overwhelm—brown tenements thorax
night's lightning—'facing'?

_____

peering on dams
crowds

_____

ill ordinary people as entire weight's
sloughs—'no' 'night'

space—occurs 1.2 billion—land is on them
only

————————

kindness—'s—mountain

a man—the rib cage warm—on his side—night's 'not'—thorax not
filled [ever] (whether 'brown' or not, night)—one's

one's

[and] is

————————

too—his night—on his side
one—'by' him (being)—thorax

[beating]. lightning [not at the same time]

————————

weight is kindness [and] 'no' night occurring
a man's side—as 'by'—black humps moon
there?

—'facing'—coal humps river

people crawling lines on coal
are

————————

to bring two huge realms—outside one—together—using the tiniest
flimsy mode.

————————

peering on dams—crowds as we pass through on a ship lightning [not at the same time] no disorder occurs, one's rim
isn't in one—(both large and small is rim)
they—

are (as 'past' pair—as peering on dams)—

———————

birds falls horizontal in the period when birds are up—[and] one is.

people not speaking—even—when—[as] birds horizontal (now)—[or are]

[past] falls horizontal (space) is people—

———————

she is in 'the realm of death' when she died   but isn't now
—my mind is phenomena—as space in my dream—existing 'only'

—being 'on' water (past) now?—as her not being—is—one—now-existing only

—is myself now, walking on water (past) in brown night there [on water]?—only—at the same time—?

—'extreme' is existing only
thinking [my] the man had died was inaccurate—as the dream. It was my grandmother wasn't (dead)

[that being happiness—as the dream being]—one isn't in death except when one died

———————

—['no'] crowds—spouts pouring
on dams

shores pouring spouts where people are

ships lightning rim

_____

ones—rainless humps
black

that are in their crawling lines?
moon

_____

dislocation of rim—peering on dams

by one

_____

black humps mountains
moon

kindness—'s—man's

lines night

_____

"white green"—'no'—occur in one in dream in a forest
walking—there not to be any—separation between 'that'—being in
forest—there
only—but the dream is "whitish" rim, 'no eyes'—there—isn't in one
—is in the dream.—pair only—are 'that'.—"white green" night—is.

the two huge realms—not in one—occur

_____

I feel I'm in a slingshot—a loop

is.

there's
no relation to ones eyes—

just go out.

*

starry sky—'to'

people

_____

one on red grass and train
is too

out there

low floating high day indigo 'to'

them red grass train

_____

buttocks into evening walking at—/separate—evening

the flaps of the orchids at evening—not running—thighs

—then—[not at the same time]—'walk'

_____

fireworks on blackness-field—not train's sound [at the same time]

breathing separated from field

_____

to' indigo

which is people

————

·   evening

people are—crawling lines night—

————

rest in my arms

[and] indigo 'no' humps lines night 'there'

————

the mind going after oneself
seen for the first time before me
is formed even—

helping one seeing the isolated self

other one isn't in lines crawling

one isn't either being that other
one nor their not being there then

[at the same time]

————

other one isn't in lines crawling

or *is*

————

other can't not be there then
[which is 'at the same time']

and one rest in my arms

indigo [and] lines 'there'

crawling on coal night [here] then
other one

————————

humps water
[not at the same time] then
lines night

['*to*' *Lyn*]

————————

Saint Colombe—which is—so—
grave and light—at the same time

cello is mounds night
————————
long thighs

operating grass orchids

apart
————————
labor orchid lines nights—go out

—[night]—the neck—coal lines—

'walk' 'then'—in evening—

————————

coal lines while living

[I feel I'm in a slingshot]

—————

'walk'—gap—one—

orchid coal lines evening

space—in them?

—————

gray and soft 'no' red indigo
no 'walk' to people

'they' (only they) 'walk'—only—which is
to 'there'—in front—one

'orchids' 'evening' 'walk'

—————

coal evening

crawl thighs

'
—————

   their thrown sack—buttocks at night in lightning is only—[as] 'in' dim
night

   buttocks [and] on both ends of one, in night 'at' lightning dim 'only
sky' not the same [as] night

   catching—arms dim night lightened—/illumined

—————

—one

buttocks in ones sack lightning—not dim nights

both.

————

both.

horizontal beside buttocks on limbs dim night. too.

————

resting lightning that is night. at all.

beside limbs buttocks both.

where one is just going out.

————

white night-trees lightning horizontal night beside

one—catching other sack who has leapt—outside of—is beside

in the future—limbs on dim night 'at' one

————

white night-tree is 'at' buttocks—both night

breathing isn't 'at' yet beside white night-tree is windless lightning

————

ones is 'the same' as night-trees—then while

not in lightning—in one

————

port as in night 'or' [which is only] one

people have space in them 'there' or only here, now
crawling lines

night is at the port—'at' one

————————

from fireflies. by people in thunder.

in blackness-rain—breathing separated

————————

   walking fireflies

   walking fireflies suspended blackness-rain—one

   people's suspended whining-hysterics—'to'—suspending leap 'ones'

   walking 'on' fireflies people in blackness-rain

   (what difference do 'people' make?)

   [fireflies are ahead] walking 'on'—suspending 'them' blackness sepa-
rated leapt—ones

————————

      for Taylor Davis
   thighs aren't any place for them

   [board is with in one.]

   mirror which is behind (not reflecting or seeing) board no kneeling or
windows fireflies

   no kneeling fireflies thighs — ones

[also] 'at' orchids   .

ones-fireflies.

thighs. 'no' neck in night.

————

people's blackness-rain not being any beside [at the same time]

being beside not being any—people as 'leapt'—and beside—'one'

green being blackness-rain / none—'to' one—they are.

skating killing depredations green

fireflies walking green—ones

————

evening running right toward 'people' not thighs—ones

'in' evening orchids ones legs and feet right toward people

banks river having walked on water 'past' lines orchids

why is running right toward people isn't one—[and] is river—blackness being

toward 'only' and that being orchids flaps [when 'past' people]—when one runs toward

green as night is unmarked

ones run toward—'people'—'at' night-greenery there—

Note

Friendship is a spatial syntax, as if rendering interior that is 'oneself' which is (also) being rendered as space of actual geographical location. It's space-based, written in China while on the Yangtze River and while here.

Though geographical space was determining the space that is one's (present) apprehension as the syntax: a different space occurs that is outside mind—also—by being (within) it.

In the whole text that is *The Public World*, the intention is to propose observation of one's own culture by superimposing 'outside' on it. *Friendship* is an 'outside' geography (in Asia, in this case) rendered as one's interior spatial sense. Land as thought.

'One' is not obliterated by land.

Geography cultural analysis as rendered/filtered only interiorly—is here scrutiny. Using geographical location (as only configuration, that is, spatial conceptualization/syntax) *Friendship* is the converse of definition *by* place. Time as being—syntactically impermanence. (See "'Thinking Serially' in *For Love, Words,* and *Pieces.*")

UNIVERSITY PRESS OF NEW ENGLAND publishes books under its own imprint and is the publisher for Brandeis University Press, Dartmouth College, Middlebury College Press, University of New Hampshire, Tufts University, and Wesleyan University Press.

ABOUT THE AUTHOR Leslie Scalapino is the author of numerous books of poetry, essays, and plays, as well as the novel *Defoe* (Sun & Moon, 1994). Among her books of poetry are *way* (1988), *that they were at the beach—aeolotropic series* (1985), and *Considering how exaggerated music is* (1982), all published with North Point Press, and *The Front Matter, Dead Souls* (1996) published with Wesleyan. Her book of poetry *New Time* was published with Wesleyan in 1999.

Library of Congress Cataloging-in-Publication Data
Scalapino, Leslie.
    The public world / syntactically impermanence / by Leslie Scalapino.
      p.   cm.
    ISBN 0–8195–6378–1 (alk. paper). ISBN 0–8195–6379–X (pbk. :
alk. paper)
    I. Title.
PS3569.C25P82 1999
811'.54–dc21   99–18712